LeBron James

Matt Christopher®

The #1 Sports Series for Kids

LITTLE, BROWN AND COMPANY
New York   Boston

Little, Brown and Company

Hachette Book Group
1290 Avenue of the Americas, New York, NY 10104
Visit us at lb-kids.com

mattchristopher.com

Little, Brown and Company is a division of Hachette Book Group, Inc.
The Little, Brown name and logo are trademarks of Hachette Book Group, Inc.

The publisher is not responsible for websites (or their content)
that are not owned by the publisher.

First Edition: September 2008

Matt Christopher® is a registered trademark of Matt Christopher Royalties, Inc.

Text written by Stephanie True Peters
Additional text written by Zachary Rau

Cover photograph by Christian Petersen/Getty Images

Library of Congress Cataloging-in-Publication Data

Christopher, Matt.
   On the court with . . . LeBron James / Matt Christopher. — 1st ed.
      p. cm. — (On the court with . . .)
   ISBN 978-0-316-01630-8
      1. James, LeBron — Juvenile literature.   2. Basketball players — United
States — Biography — Juvenile literature.   I. Title.
   GV884.J36C47 2008
   796.323092 — dc22
   [B]
                                                          2008010593

10

LSC-C

Printed in the United States of America

Contents

⋆ PROLOGUE ⋆

To look at him now, you might not think that LeBron James was once like lots of kids in the United States. But he was. He went to school, played sports, and hung out with his friends. He did chores. He watched television and played video games. He worshipped sports heroes such as Michael Jordan.

LeBron was like many kids in the U.S. in other ways, too. His mother was a single working woman struggling to make ends meet. He never knew his father. Throughout much of his childhood, he lived in neighborhoods where crime, violence, and drug use were the norm.

Yet he was different, too. For one thing, he was tall, taller than most other boys his age. But it was when he picked up a basketball and strode onto the court that his true difference emerged — for that young boy could do things with a basketball that few others could.

Still can.

★ CHAPTER ONE ★

1984–1987

Hickory Street

LeBron James was born on December 30, 1984. His mother, Gloria James, was a sixteen-year-old high school student and unmarried. No one has ever known for certain who his father was.

LeBron and Gloria lived with her mother, Freda, and Gloria's two brothers, Terry and Curt, in a small house on Hickory Street in Akron, Ohio. Hickory Street was in one of Akron's poorer neighborhoods. Sometimes, homes in such areas can fall into disrepair. The neighborhoods themselves can become crime-ridden and dangerous.

Not so with Hickory Street. The residents there kept their homes neat. If a person or family was in need, neighbors stepped forward with food, shelter, clothes, or other help. The people there may not have had much, but what they had they were glad to share, because they knew that someday, they might be the ones who needed help.

Freda, Gloria, Terry, and even Curt, who was only nine when Gloria's baby was born, worked hard to give LeBron all the love and care he needed. It wasn't easy, for money was tight and newborns can be challenging. But they made it work all the same.

They soon had another set of hands to help out. When LeBron was eight months old, Gloria began dating a man named Eddie Jackson. Eddie was twenty years old and struggling to find his direction in life. Freda helped him by giving him a place in her home with her children and grandson.

Not all twenty-year-old men are comfortable around babies, but Eddie took to LeBron right away. In fact, he is the only man LeBron has ever called Dad.

LeBron quickly grew from an infant to an active toddler. Jumping, running, tackling — he was in constant motion. "You could be laying on the floor," Eddie once recalled, "and the next thing you know . . . he'd jump right on you."

So much energy needed an outlet. So, for Christmas just before LeBron's third birthday, Eddie and Gloria purchased a child-sized basketball hoop and ball. They set it up near the tree on Christmas Eve.

But that night, tragedy struck. Around three o'clock, Freda James collapsed in her kitchen. Eddie heard her fall and came running. He shouted for Gloria to

4

call for help. But it was too late. Freda died in his arms within minutes.

Gloria, Eddie, Terry, and Curt were grief-stricken. Yet with great effort, they hid their sorrow from little LeBron that Christmas morning.

"We wanted to make things as normal for him as possible," Eddie later said. "He had no idea that his grandmother had died."

Indeed, photographs they took that day show LeBron laughing and enjoying the wonder of the holiday. They also show him playing with his brand-new basketball set. At first, he didn't really know how to use it properly. Instead of tossing the ball into the hoop, he rammed it through the rim with fierce slam dunks.

Gloria and Eddie raised the hoop to its highest level, thinking it would encourage LeBron to try shooting. Instead, as the family watched half amused, half amazed, LeBron simply took a running leap and stuffed the ball.

"I was thinking, 'Man, this kid has some elevation for just being three years old,'" Eddie remembered.

LeBron's happiness that Christmas morning was a welcome distraction from the grief the others were feeling over Freda's death. But when the holidays were over, the reality of their loss and their situation set in.

Freda had been the glue that held the family together. Without her, things slowly fell apart.

Eddie, Terry, and Gloria, scarcely more than children themselves, struggled to take care of twelve-year-old Curt and three-year-old LeBron. Their Hickory Street neighbors helped with meals and child care, but there was only so much they could do. And there was nothing anyone could do to help the James children overcome their grief.

As for the house, none of them had the time, money, or know-how to properly care for it. Before long, the dwelling fell into disrepair. Then the city had it condemned — and eventually torn down.

Without a roof over their heads, Gloria, LeBron, and the others were forced to search for other places to live — or else take to the streets, homeless.

✷ CHAPTER TWO ✷

1987–1994

LeBron and Gloria

In the wake of Freda's death and the loss of the Hickory Street house, the James family had no choice but to split up. Terry and Curt left together to find a new place to live. Eddie, who was no longer dating Gloria, moved in with his aunt.

Gloria and LeBron, meanwhile, moved to Elizabeth Park. Elizabeth Park was located in a rough, crime-ridden area where the wail of police sirens often woke residents in the middle of the night.

"I saw drugs, guns, killings," LeBron later recalled. "It was crazy."

But Elizabeth Park was also where many of Gloria's friends lived, people who opened their homes to her and her son. Gloria couldn't afford a place of her own, so when someone offered them a room to sleep in, she accepted gratefully.

They didn't stay with one set of friends for more than a few months, however. "My mom would always say,

'Don't get comfortable, because we may not be here long,'" LeBron remembered, adding that when he was five years old, they moved seven times.

Adjusting to such an unsettled existence wasn't easy for either of them. But somehow, Gloria managed to make it work. "My mom kept food in my mouth and clothes on my back," LeBron said years later.

Not surprisingly, LeBron found the violence in and around Elizabeth Park terrifying. Equally frightening was the fact that youngsters not much older than him were sometimes involved in the crimes.

But he himself never got in trouble. "That just wasn't me," he has said. "I knew it was wrong."

LeBron didn't have many close friends back then because he and Gloria moved around so much. Attending school regularly was difficult for him, too. In fact, when he was in the fourth grade, he missed more than eighty days of school!

Fortunately, around this same time, LeBron found a new lifeline in the form of organized sports. In 1994, he joined a football team, the South Rangers, in Akron's Pee Wee League. Attending practices, learning the rules, playing the game, making friends — nine-year-old LeBron loved everything about football and being part of a team.

"The South Rangers meant a lot to me," he said. "All

the coaches and the parents really cared about us. I actually wanted to play in the NFL."

Such a dream wasn't that far-fetched, for LeBron was a terrific player, one whose prowess on the field got him attention.

Frankie Walker Sr. was one of the people who noticed LeBron. Walker had once played for the South Rangers himself and still enjoyed following his old team's schedule. He befriended LeBron and Gloria. When he learned about LeBron's long absences from school, he realized the pair's erratic home life was causing trouble for the youngster.

Walker didn't want LeBron to be one of those kids who fell through the cracks, so he approached Gloria with an unusual proposal. He, his wife, Pam, and their three children wanted LeBron to come live with them.

It was to be a temporary situation, he assured Gloria, just until she was settled somewhere. If she agreed, LeBron would be treated as a member of their family. He would have regular meals, a structured schedule that included attending school regularly and doing household chores, plus the comfort of a nice home and the support of people who cared about him.

Gloria saw that the Walkers were good people and that LeBron liked and trusted them as much as she did.

So, with the knowledge that she and LeBron would be together most weekends, she agreed to let LeBron go live with the Walkers.

The arrangement proved life-changing for LeBron. Under the Walkers' care, he settled into a routine that provided him with more stability than he had ever known.

"They are like my family," LeBron says today, "and I wouldn't be here without them."

It was while living with the Walkers that he returned to a sport he'd first tried when he was just two years old: basketball.

★ CHAPTER THREE ★

1994–1998

Honing His Talent

Frankie Walker Sr. coached a youth basketball team, the Summit Lake Hornets, at the local community recreation center. His son, Frankie Jr., was a member of the squad. When LeBron joined the Walker household, he joined the team, too.

Frankie Jr. was a good player, in part because he was naturally talented and in part because his father had been coaching him for a long time. At first, he beat LeBron every time they played a game of one-on-one.

But LeBron was a quick study. As he learned the rules of the game, how to move with the ball, and how to shoot, he drew even with Frankie Jr. and eventually surpassed him.

Frankie Sr. had seen many skilled players in his time, but LeBron's growing talent amazed him. "He doesn't golf," he once commented, "but if he picked up some golf clubs, Tiger Woods better watch out."

Walker was impressed by LeBron's sportsmanship, too. Sometimes young players sulk, blame their teammates, or bad-mouth their opponents when they lose. Not LeBron. Instead of moaning about a loss, he'd practice harder so he'd do better next time.

But what Walker found most intriguing about LeBron wasn't his skill or attitude. It was his knack for "seeing" how the action on the court was going to unfold.

While other players often scrambled to follow what was happening during games, LeBron seemed to anticipate what was going to happen next. He wasn't seeing into the future, just making accurate guesses about where the ball would go, how players would move, and where the next open shot would be. And then he would act on his instincts and move to catch the pass, make the block, dish the assist, or take the shot.

No one taught him how to do this because it's not something that can be taught. You either have it, or you don't. And LeBron had it, big-time.

"The game came naturally to me," LeBron once told *Sports Illustrated for Kids*.

Helping others learn that game came naturally, too, it turned out. Walker was so impressed by LeBron's play and sportsmanship that at the start of the 1995 season, he asked LeBron, now a fifth grader, to help coach his fourth-grade team. LeBron agreed and soon was dividing his court time between playing for his own team and assisting Walker on the sidelines.

Juggling two basketball schedules was tricky, especially when school, homework, and household chores were thrown into the mix. Before moving in with the Walkers, LeBron hadn't taken such duties seriously. Homework, in particular, had taken a backseat to video games and other playtime activities.

But in the fifth grade, that began to change. The Walkers' discipline played a part in LeBron's new attitude toward his responsibilities. But it was LeBron himself who really made the difference.

"It [got] to me," he once admitted. "When you know you'll be the only one not turning in [the homework], it doesn't feel right."

There were other reasons LeBron wanted to keep up with his schoolwork. If his grades started to slide, he wouldn't be allowed to play sports. But more importantly, he wanted to set a good example for the fourth-grade boys he was helping coach. He realized he was a role model to them; if he slacked off in school, they might, too. But if he gave schoolwork his all, maybe they would try their hardest there as well.

LeBron stayed with the Walkers through 1994 and into 1995. He was grateful for their kindness and generosity, yet he couldn't help but hope that one day, he and his mother would be together again as their own family.

His hope was realized in 1995, when Gloria found a steady job and a permanent home for them in a neighborhood called Spring Hill. Eleven-year-old LeBron moved out of the Walkers' home and into the two-bedroom apartment where he and Gloria would live for the next seven years. He attended Reidinger Middle School, where he made good friends and kept up with his homework. He played sports, too: football in the fall and basketball in the winter, spring, and summer.

In 1996, LeBron joined an Amateur Athletic Union (AAU) basketball team called the Shooting Stars. His coach was Dru Joyce II, a man who played a huge part in his basketball career that year and in years to come — as did three of his new teammates: Joyce's son, Dru III, or Little Dru as he was known; Sian Cotton; and Willie McGee.

At five feet six inches, Little Dru was small like his nickname, but dynamite on the court. Sian was a chunky jokester, but surprisingly athletic for his size. Willie was a quiet, considerate boy who had originally played on another team before being invited to join the Shooting Stars by Coach Dru.

When LeBron, Little Dru, Sian, and Willie began to play together, something special happened. Almost from the beginning, the Fab Four, as they called themselves, was a force to be reckoned with.

"Every year they were together," Coach Dru remembered, "they placed in the top ten of the AAU national championship. Except when they were thirteen," he added, "they had a big head and they didn't place. But they came back the next year at fourteen."

In all, when their AAU careers drew to a close in 1999, the Shooting Stars had won six national championships and more than two hundred games.

Those years of AAU ball helped LeBron hone his skills on the court and develop as a team player. They also gave him plenty of experience traveling out-of-state — something LeBron had never done before and that he found very scary at first. (Coach Dru recalls that LeBron cried throughout his first plane ride!) Those tournaments were instrumental in furthering LeBron as a player, for they gave him his first taste of competition at the national level. But best of all, the time he and his teammates shared on the road cemented friendships that would endure for years to come.

"They believed in themselves and each other," Coach Dru said of his crackerjack squad.

As their final AAU season wound down, LeBron and his friends realized they wanted to continue playing ball together in high school. But which high school?

Akron allowed students to choose their high school. Most people assumed they would select Buchtel High School, not only because it was close to their homes but because Coach Dru was the assistant coach of the varsity basketball team there.

But to everyone else's surprise, the Fab Four had made a different choice. Their decision centered around an unlikely person: a former college basketball coach who had once been blacklisted from the sport because of a racial scandal.

⋆ CHAPTER FOUR ⋆

1999–2000

"Unreal"

In January 1993, Coach Keith Dambrot of Central Michigan University's Division I basketball team called his team into the locker room for a halftime pep talk. During the talk, he used a word that can be extremely offensive to African-Americans. When the media found out, he was denounced as a racist. In April, he was fired.

Dambrot tried to explain that he hadn't used the word to offend anyone. He apologized, admitted to making a mistake, and pointed out that as a Jew, he himself knew how hurtful slurs can be.

Nothing he said mattered. He was out of a job and for years afterward, no one in the basketball world wanted anything to do with him.

Then in 1997, a Jewish community center in Akron gave him permission to hold Sunday basketball clinics. Among those who attended the clinic's first sessions was Dru Joyce III, then in eighth grade. A few

17

Sundays later, Little Dru brought his friends Sian, Willie, and LeBron. From there on out, the foursome rarely missed Dambrot's clinics.

The Fab Four were impressed with Dambrot's coaching abilities. Their parents were, too. They knew all about Dambrot's past but unlike some, they were willing to give him another chance, particularly when they saw how good he was with their children.

"Keith is my man," Gloria James put it simply. "He's alright."

Dambrot impressed other people, too, including the staff of a small Catholic high school. In 1998, St. Vincent-St. Mary High School (SVSM) was looking for a new varsity basketball coach. Dambrot got the job; during his first season as coach, he led the team to one of the best records they'd had in years.

When the Fab Four finished their last AAU season, they realized they all wanted the same thing: to play ball together on Dambrot's team. So when the time came, they choose SVSM as their high school.

Their decision surprised many. SVSM had a good athletics program, but it was not known as a sports school. Instead, its focus was on academics. Some speculated that the boys' budding basketball careers would flounder there.

The boys thought otherwise. In fact, they believed going to SVSM would keep them from being lost in the shuffle at a much larger, sports-oriented public school. They would also be getting an excellent education there.

So it was that LeBron James entered SVSM as a freshman in 1999. Standing at six feet, four inches tall and weighing in at 170 pounds, he towered over most of the student body and many of the staff as well. But he gained his first real notice as a member of one of the school's teams — although not, as one might expect, as a basketball player. Not at first, anyway.

In the fall of 1999, LeBron started out as a wide receiver on the Fighting Irish freshman football team. He played so well that the varsity coaches promoted him to their squad midway through the season. He didn't play much there because most of the passes were thrown to a talented senior named Maverick Carter.

Still, in the last quarter of the last game of the season, LeBron showed just how effective he could be. The Fighting Irish needed to win the game in order to go into the postseason. LeBron did all he could to help them by catching nine passes. Unfortunately, the Irish still lost by two points.

Soon after that game, basketball season began. All of the Fab Four made Dambrot's team, but almost from the start, LeBron stood out from the others. He was a competitive player who used his height and weight to muscle his way under the basket, his quickness to work around slower players, and his heads-up play to create scoring opportunities. He helped the team win their first game by chalking up 15 points; by the end of the regular schedule, he and the Fighting Irish were undefeated.

The team powered through the postseason as well to reach the Division III state championship game. There they came up against Jamestown Greeneview High School. Greeneview's record of 23–5 was not as good as St. Vincent's but still, there was no guarantee that St. Vincent would win.

No guarantee other than the exceptional play of a freshman guard named LeBron James, that is. In the course of that game, played on March 25, 2000, thirteen thousand people got a look at the future of basketball when he hit the court.

Sporting number 32, the reverse of his favorite NBA player, Michael Jordan, LeBron drained 25 points, ripped down 9 rebounds, and dished out 4 assists.

Yet as good as LeBron's stats were, the real hero of the game was fifteen-year-old Little Dru. He came off the bench and proceeded to hit an astonishing seven out of seven three-point shots! As the last seconds ticked down, shouts of "Druuuuu!" echoed through the stands.

Between the two of them, Little Dru and LeBron accounted for more than half of the team's 73 points that night. The Fighting Irish won the match to become the Division III Ohio State Champions, their first title since 1984. Fittingly, after the game, Dru Joyce III was the center of attention. And no one was happier for him than LeBron and the other Fab Four.

LeBron ended the season with impressive statistics for a freshman. He had averaged 18 points per game and 6.2 rebounds. But more important than those numbers was the fact that he was developing into a true team player.

"LeBron would go get 15 points against a bad team," Coach Dambrot once noted, "but would make sure everybody else was getting into the game."

Assistant coach Steven Culp was even more enthusiastic. "This kid," he predicted, "is going to be unreal."

★ CHAPTER FIVE ★

2000–2001

Sophomore Sensation

In the summer between his freshman and sophomore years in high school, LeBron was given two unique opportunities to showcase his basketball talent.

The first was at the Slam-N-Jam AAU tournament in California. There, he played on a team called Soldiers I. After a shaky start, he helped the Soldiers win three games in a row.

"He was phenomenal," said Calvin Andrews, then head of the tournament.

A few weeks later, LeBron traveled closer to home, to Pittsburgh, Pennsylvania, to attend the highly respected Five-Star basketball camp.

Five-Star was founded in 1966 by Howard Garfinkel, one of basketball's premier scouts. In the decades that followed, Garfinkel and the coaches of Five-Star honed the skills of many players who went on to become some of the biggest names in college and professional basketball. Michael Jordan, Grant Hill, Alonzo

Mourning: Garfinkel had seen his share of young, raw talent every summer at Five-Star.

In Garfinkel's opinion, LeBron James showed the potential to blow every one of them out of the water.

"I've never seen anything quite like it," he said when he first watched LeBron in action.

That week at Five-Star, LeBron worked on his basketball game as never before. Shooting drills, passing drills, offense, defense, game play — nothing was left out. The experience showed him what he was capable of, what he needed to work on, and who he might one day play with or against if his basketball career reached the college or professional level.

But that day was a long way off, for LeBron still had three years of high school left to finish.

His sophomore year at SVSM began differently than the previous one. Then he had been a nervous, larger-than-average-sized freshman trying to figure out the lay of the school and how he fit in. Now he walked in as one of the most recognized figures on campus, a star athlete and a well-liked member of the student body.

LeBron's fall semester was filled with schoolwork, homework, and best of all, football. This year, he was the go-to wide receiver on the team, a position vacated with the graduation of his good friend Maverick Carter. LeBron filled the position admirably. Even when he was double- or triple-teamed, he made spectacular catches. He used his speed and agility to outpace and dodge around the defense and his muscle to power past and in some cases, over, his opponents. By the season's end, he had snatched 42 passes from the air for 840 yards and 11 touchdowns. For his efforts, he earned a place on the Division VI All-Ohio first team.

Next up was basketball. LeBron, Little Dru, Sian, and Willie were looking forward to another stellar year, the fifth they would play together as teammates. But this season, something was different. The Fab Four was about to add a new member, a transfer student named Romeo Travis.

Romeo didn't fit in with the other four right away, but fortunately, whatever conflicts they had before the season were behind them by the time they hit the courts. The five played together like a well-oiled machine. With solid support from the bench, the Fighting Irish racked up 27 wins during the regular season while giving up only one game.

Most players would have been very happy with such a good record. But that single mid-season loss hit LeBron very hard.

The match was against Oak Hill Academy of Virginia, the top-ranked Division III high school team in the country. Originally scheduled to be played at SVSM's gym, the game had to be moved to the arena at nearby Ohio State University in Columbus because demand for tickets was so high. More than ten thousand spectators showed up to see the two teams duke it out. Members of the media were there, too, not only to report on the game but to see LeBron James, the rising star of Ohio's high school circuit.

And LeBron did not disappoint. From the moment he stepped onto the floor and assumed his small forward position, he played his heart out. Spurred on by his efforts, the Fighting Irish led 52–42 going into the third quarter. A win seemed in the bag.

But Oak Hill wasn't the number-one team for no reason. They chopped SVSM's lead to seven with three minutes left in the game.

Then disaster struck. LeBron got a cramp and was forced to sit out until the pain subsided. He returned quickly — perhaps too quickly, for he seemed off his game and failed to hit a 13-foot jumper and two free throws in the final minute.

The Oak Hill Warriors, meanwhile, had pulled ahead by a single point. Then, with the score 79–78 and the final seconds ticking off the clock, LeBron got the ball. He launched a buzzer-beating three-point attempt — and missed.

Oak Hill's one-point victory ended SVSM's two-season, 36-game winning streak. It also left LeBron devastated. After the game, he sat slumped on the floor, head down, arms on bent knees, and eyes full of tears.

Fortunately for the Irish, their star player put the loss behind him. "It hurts," LeBron told reporters later, "but we got all the tears and the frustration and the disappointment out of our system and it's time to get back to work."

And work he did! He went on to have the best season of any sophomore in the state of Ohio, scoring 20 or more points and averaging more than seven rebounds per game. With LeBron spearheading the charge, SVSM powered through the postseason to capture their second consecutive Division III state championship.

That final game was played against Casstown Miami East on March 24, 2001. LeBron scored 25 points in the 63–53 victory; to no one's surprise, he was named MVP and chosen for the all-state team after the win.

Those last points brought LeBron's year-end average to 25.2 per game. He also averaged 7.2 rebounds, 5.8 assists, and 2.38 steals — astonishing statistics for any player, let alone a fifteen-year-old high school sophomore!

In fact, his season-long performance was so impressive that he was named *The Sporting News* high school sophomore player of the year. He was also awarded Ohio's Mr. Basketball title, given to the best player in the state, and, later, named to *USA Today*'s

All-American team. It was the first time those two honors had ever been given to a sophomore.

On the surface, everything seemed to be going smoothly for LeBron and the Fighting Irish. But big changes were in the works. After three successful years as head coach of SVSM, Keith Dambrot announced that he was leaving to pursue a college opportunity.

LeBron, Sian, Willie, Romeo, Little Dru, and the rest of the team were understandably upset by the news. With Dambrot at the helm, they had won two state championships and lost just one game in two seasons. Who, they wondered, could possibly fill his shoes?

As it turned out, the answer to that question was better than they could have hoped for. Starting in the fall of 2001, their new head coach would be one of their team's assistant coaches — none other than Dru Joyce II, Little Dru's father.

"I think we'll be alright," LeBron predicted soon after the announcement. "We're gonna do what we've been doing the past two years. We're 53–1. We gotta keep doing it."

But of course, only time would tell if Coach Dru could guide his players to those same heights — and help the team's star forward continue to rise.

★ CHAPTER SIX ★

2001–2002

"The Chosen One"

The summer after his freshman year in high school, LeBron James had gone to the Five-Star camp as a relative unknown. He showed great promise but was still considered to be too young and inexperienced to warrant more than passing interest.

When LeBron set off to begin a series of summer basketball camps between his sophomore and junior years, however, it was a completely different story. He was the one most people were watching, and not just because of his ability. In addition to his spectacular statistics, he was a real presence on the court, for he weighed 225 pounds and stood six feet, seven inches tall!

His first summer stop was Colorado Springs for the USA Basketball Youth Development Festival. LeBron was one of forty high school players to participate — and the first underclassman ever to receive an invitation to the four-day Festival. He proved he belonged there by averaging 24 points and chalking up 120 points in five games to break the existing Festival record. His performance earned him the MVP award.

Soon afterward, LeBron traveled across the country to Teaneck, New Jersey, for the adidas ABCD Camp. Founded by basketball shoe executive Sonny Vaccaro, the camp boasted the sport's top high school players. One of those players was a senior from Brooklyn, New York, named Lenny Cooke.

Cooke was considered *the* hot prospect; many colleges and NBA scouts had come to the camp to watch him play. They also looked forward to seeing how LeBron would fare against the older, more experienced player when their respective teams met for a game.

It turned out to be no contest. LeBron outscored Lenny 24 points to 9, including a three-pointer made on the fly at the buzzer that won the game 85–83. Anyone who didn't know about LeBron James before that shot sure knew about him after it.

"This was the first time LeBron really emerged," commented Vaccaro. "He clearly beat the number-one player in the country."

LeBron himself was fairly nonchalant about his play in a match some had billed as the Game of the Century. "I just wanted to give everyone a good show," he said.

He continued to give "good shows" when he returned to SVSM a few months later. First came football, where his great height, nimble moves, and powerful muscles helped him nab 52 receptions for 11 touchdowns and more than 1,000 yards. Bolstered by his play, the Fighting Irish made it into the playoffs.

Ohio football fans loved LeBron, colleges and universities were drooling over him, and the NFL kept careful watch over his every move. Everyone, LeBron included, hoped he would continue playing football.

Everyone except his mother, that is. Gloria knew that her son loved playing football and that he had great skill in the sport. But she believed his future was in basketball. Before his junior year, she had tried to convince him not to play football. She was worried he might be badly injured and thus ruin his chances for a basketball career.

Her concerns turned out to have some merit, for in the very first game in the postseason, LeBron fractured the index finger on his left hand. He kept mum about the injury and when the Irish won that first game to go on to the finals, he suited up and took to the field as if nothing was wrong.

That game, a SVSM loss, was his last as a football player. Although his finger wasn't troubling him too much, he knew he had been lucky that the injury wasn't any worse. He realized his mother was right: at this point, it would be foolhardy to do anything that might jeopardize his future in basketball.

By some accounts, that future wasn't all that far away. Unbelievably, rumors had started to fly that LeBron was considering a jump to the NBA — *before* completing his junior year in high school!

The sixteen-year-old squashed those rumors almost as soon as they began. "That is not going to happen," he told the press firmly. "I can do more to get my brain and my game ready if I finish school."

LeBron had other reasons for staying in school besides completing his education. He wanted to add a third and a fourth state championship to the two he and the Fighting Irish had already won. He also hoped to win a national championship.

Such dreams weren't far-fetched. Under the direction of Dru Joyce II, the Fab Five and their teammates rolled over the competition to a 7–1 record by the end of December.

LeBron was the main reason for the team's success. He was regularly shooting 25 to 35 points each game and racking up solid numbers in rebounds, assists, and steals as well. As the season progressed, the whispers about him grew from low murmurs to animated discussions to excited cries. Then, in mid-Feburary of 2002, they turned into out-and-out roars of approval.

That month, *Sports Illustrated* featured LeBron

James on its cover. The magazine had put high school students on the cover in the past, but LeBron was the first underclassman to be in that spot. But even more remarkable was the tagline that accompanied his picture: "The Chosen One." With those three simple words, LeBron James, who had turned seventeen just a month and a half earlier, was officially hailed as the future of the NBA, a position once held by his hero, Michael Jordan.

The magazine flew off the stands. Hundreds of issues flooded SVSM's front office and people brandishing copies appeared out of nowhere, all with requests for LeBron's signature.

"Everybody comes up to me, all these grown folks, asking for autographs, talking about it's for their kids," LeBron commented, half-amused, half-annoyed. "Next thing you know, they're selling it on eBay."

In the end, LeBron refused to sign any magazines unless he knew who he was signing it for, a wise move considering that copies of the autographed covers did indeed start selling on the Internet, some for as much as two hundred dollars!

The *Sports Illustrated* story gained LeBron national attention. But he was already famous at home. Ticket sales had been brisk ever since he started playing as a freshman. But now, they were so strong that many home games had to be played at the University of

Akron arena. Prices sometimes reached seventy-five dollars — and many fans insisted on purchasing season tickets!

Rarely had there been such frenzy over a high school player. Only Kobe Bryant, Tracy McGrady, and Kevin Garrett, three outstanding basketball stars who had jumped straight from high school to the NBA, had garnered as much attention and enthusiasm.

Some basketball insiders wondered if the pressure of being in such a bright spotlight would prove to be too much for the seventeen-year-old. "[Instant fame] ruined a lot of kids who couldn't handle it," Howard Garfinkel of Five-Star pointed out once.

For the most part, LeBron didn't seem distracted by the attention. With regular season averages of 28 points, 6 assists, and just under 9 rebounds, he led his team to a 23–4 record and a playoff berth for the third year in a row. There, they dribbled and shot their way to the final round to face the Spartans from Roger Bacon High School of Cincinnati, Ohio.

The Fighting Irish had beaten the Spartans earlier in the season in a hard-fought game. This rematch, played before a crowd of 18,375 spectators (many of whom had paid $150 for a ticket!) was to be equally close.

The two teams traded the lead throughout the first half. But then, in the third quarter, the Irish fell behind.

With four minutes left in the game, they saw the Spartans pull away, 48 to 37.

Then LeBron, who had seemed to struggle this game and was rumored to be suffering from back spasms, came alive. First he rolled in three layups. Then he catapulted a 40-foot jumper right as time on the shot clock ran out. Those points brought the Irish to within five of the Spartans.

Roger Bacon didn't let up, though. With little more than two minutes left in the game, they scored enough to stay in the lead by four.

Then, with 2:17 remaining, LeBron cut that lead by two with yet another layup. Spartans 60, Irish 58.

Less than a minute later, however, the Spartans were up by five.

Once more, LeBron took over. With 1:20 on the clock, he slammed in a thunderous dunk to draw within three. But the Spartans answered with two points of their own to pull ahead by five again.

To close a five-point gap so close to the end of a game requires great playing by all team members. LeBron did his part with a three-point play with thirty seconds remaining to make it 65–63. If the Irish scored just one more bucket, they would send the game into overtime. If they put in three points, they would win. In such a position, they did what any sensible team would do — they got the ball to their best player, LeBron James.

LeBron dribbled down court. Spartan defenders jumped in front of him to block any attempted shot But LeBron fooled them. He passed off to teammate Chad Mraz. Mraz spun, shot — and missed.

The Spartans crashed the boards, came down with the rebound, and scored — and then moments later, unbelievably, scored *again*.

The Fighting Irish were down by six. They had no choice now but to put a time-honored basketball strategy into play: foul the Spartans, send them to the free throw line, and hope the shooter missed the throw so they could grab the rebound and score on a fast break.

Unfortunately, the strategy backfired. The Spartan made both buckets. There was no way any team, not even one that had LeBron James, could recover.

Final score: Roger Bacon, 71, St. Vincent-St. Mary, 63.

The loss was devastating for the Fighting Irish. Many of the players left the arena in tears, wanting nothing more than to put as much distance as possible between themselves and the celebrating Spartans.

LeBron was heartbroken that his team hadn't won their third straight state championship. Not even being named the game's MVP could take away that sting. But unlike some of his teammates, he swallowed his disappointment and shook hands with every Spartan before disappearing into the locker room.

"This is only a game the way I look at it," he said later. "I'm not going to dwell on it, I'm not going to cry. The best thing for me is to wake up the next morning."

Chances are, LeBron slept in late the following morning. But the day after that, he gave many basketball outsiders a glimpse of the type of person he was off the court. That afternoon, he showed up for a scheduled appearance at a local mall to sign autographs. Many of his fans had stood in line for more than ten hours.

Although his team had lost the championship, LeBron was still their hero.

★ CHAPTER SEVEN ★

2002

"The Whole Truth"

The basketball world continued to embrace LeBron James in the months that followed the 2002 state championships. For the second year in a row, he became Ohio's Mr. Basketball. In April, he was named Gatorade's national basketball player of the year, the first high school junior to receive that honor. *Parade* magazine awarded him a similar trophy. Three weeks later, he was chosen for *USA Today*'s All-USA boys basketball team for the second straight year.

Soon after he received these awards, LeBron found himself the subject of two wild rumors about where he was going to play the next season. The first said he was planning to leave SVSM to play for Oak Hill Academy, their archrival. The other claimed he had accepted a multimillion-dollar offer to play in the pro leagues in Europe and would soon be moving to Italy. Neither rumor had any basis in fact, but that didn't stop them from spreading like a virus all the same.

Off-base speculation about his future wasn't Le-Bron's only problem that spring. At the end of May, he was invited to work out with some of the players in the Cleveland Cavaliers. James accepted — what seventeen-year-old wouldn't have? — only to learn afterward that the session was against NBA rules.

According to regulations, there can be no contact between NBA teams and players who are not yet eligible for the draft. LeBron wouldn't be eligible until his high school class graduated. For breaking that rule, the Cavs coach, John Lucas, was suspended for the first two games of the 2002–2003 season; the Cavs were also fined $150,000.

LeBron, fortunately, emerged from the scandal unscathed. Equally important, anyone who saw him practice with the Cavs agreed that he'd more than held his own against the talented professionals. "We got to have him," the impressed coach was reported to have said after watching LeBron ram in a reverse dunk.

That LeBron loved to dunk was no surprise, but in early June, one dunk gave him a huge scare. While playing in a Shooting Stars AAU game, he was tripped up by an opponent after thrusting the ball through the hoop. He fell and hit his left wrist against the floor. An exam showed the worst: the wrist was broken.

Fortunately, LeBron was a quick healer and eight weeks later he was playing as if nothing had happened.

"You can't just let up, because you never know if you're going to wake up the next day," he said matter-of-factly.

Still, had the injury been to his shooting hand, he might not have been so calm, for such a break had the potential to end his NBA career before it had even started. That everyone expected him to have an amazing NBA career — and sooner rather than later — was obvious, if only because of the bidding war that was going on for the rights to another part of his body: his foot.

Ever since Michael Jordan proved how successful celebrity sneakers could be, shoe companies had courted top players to endorse products. In the summer of 2002, both Nike and adidas began dangling promises of huge sums of money if LeBron would link his name to theirs.

LeBron held off making any decisions. Instead, he played a prank on both companies by wearing Nike gear to the adidas ABCD camp, and adidas gear to Nike's All-American camp!

Many in the media appreciated LeBron's joke. But others reported it as a sign of the teen's growing arrogance. LeBron added fuel to that fire when he showed up an hour late to a press conference. Miffed at being kept waiting, many reporters put their anger into words, calling LeBron bigheaded and conceited.

LeBron's champions quickly rose to his defense. They pointed out that the media had been the ones to label LeBron as "The Chosen One" and "The Next Michael Jordan." How could they now blame him for buying into those labels, especially when he was being hounded by the press, by eager autograph-seekers, and by shoe companies, all hungry for a piece of him?

The buzz surrounding LeBron continued to grow as he entered his senior year in high school — and when word got out that one of the Fighting Irish's basketball games was to be shown by ESPN2 on national television, it became deafening.

Never before had a high school game been broadcast live during prime-time viewing hours. But this was no ordinary game. It was St. Vincent-St. Mary vs. Oak Hill Academy, one of the hottest rivalries in high school sports. On the night of December 12, camera crews gathered in Rhodes Arena to witness a match billed as "The Futures Game."

Two legends of basketball, NBA Hall-of-Famer Bill Walton and renowned college announcer Dick Vitale, were on the scene to provide play-by-play commentary. Twelve thousand spectators, many of whom had paid upward of $75 per ticket, were in the stands; many millions more tuned in at home.

Also in the stands was Gloria James. She was — and always had been — her son's most outspoken supporter.

This game was no different. She wore her custom-made Fighting Irish jersey with the words "LeBron's Mom" emblazoned on the back and carried a small fan with her son's image on the front.

LeBron carried a sign of his bond with his mother at all times, too. On one of his biceps, he had a tattoo of the name Gloria. But since high school rules order players to cover up such markings with tape or bandages, no one there that night saw the inking. Instead, they took in LeBron's green NBA logo headband, the gold "Chosen One" band he'd put around his calf, and his green and gold adidas sneakers.

The Warriors went into the match with a record of 6–0 and the top slot in the national rankings. The Irish, on the other hand, had only two complete wins under their belts; a third game had been suspended halfway through due to a power outage. Who would come out on top was anybody's guess.

What was LeBron's impression of the upcoming match? "It's Oak Hill. This is NOT like any other game."

It certainly didn't start out like any other game for LeBron. He went for nearly five minutes without making a basket! Then, finally, with the score Oak Hill 10, SVSM 3, with 3:04 left in the first quarter, he converted an above-the-rim pass into his first two points of the night.

That alley-oop was a nice move, but overall, LeBron had not been particularly impressive so far. In fact, one online commentator claimed he was just "standing around."

That was about to change.

With just under two minutes remaining in the first quarter, the Fighting Irish stole the ball from beneath the Warriors hoop. LeBron, alone near mid-court, caught the breakaway pass.

"Uh oh! Uh oh!" commentator Dick Vitale cried excitedly as LeBron bolted for the hoop and then took off into the air.

Up, up, up, and then SLAM! LeBron delivered a monstrous tomahawk dunk!

The spectators leaped to their feet. Thunderous applause shook the bleachers. *This* was the kind of move they had come to see — and there was plenty more to come.

LeBron had six points by the end of the first quarter. A minute and a half into the second, he reached double digits with two alley-oops, the second after a sweet backdoor cut. Those four points helped close the gap between the Irish and the Warriors, but Oak Hill was still winning, 19–16.

Thirty seconds later, SVSM was within one. The points came thanks to a beautiful, no-look, behind-the-back pass from LeBron to Romeo Travis that had

Dick Vitale yelling "Are you *serious*? I got goose bumps watching that!" Travis was fouled on the missed layup but converted the free throws to bring the score to 19–18.

Less than a minute later, SVSM took their first lead of the game, 20–19, on another no-look pass assist from LeBron.

But Oak Hill hadn't become the number-one team in the country by giving up. With two minutes remaining in the first half, they tied the score — only to see their lead slip through their fingers yet again. When the buzzer sounded to end the first half, SVSM was up 30–25. LeBron was responsible for 13 of those points, as well as 5 rebounds and 4 assists.

He chalked up six more points, including two made when he snatched his own rebound, before three minutes had ticked by in the third quarter. 37–27 in favor of the Irish.

But the Warriors hadn't given up the battle. They laid siege to the Irish while surging forward with ten points of their own to tie it all up, 37–37.

SVSM quickly broke free, however, to gain a 50–43 lead going into the fourth quarter. That lead stretched to 56–43 within the first two minutes, with LeBron draining an impressive three-pointer at the 6:50 mark that had Bill Walton and Dick Vitale cheering along with the crowd.

But moments later, those cheers turned to gasps when LeBron was leveled while attempting to make a layup. He hit the floor hard, but luckily he was uninjured and jumped right back into the action.

That action, it turned out, came almost completely from SVSM's side. Oak Hill had entered the fourth quarter with 43 points total. At the five-minute mark, they hadn't added to that score — while the Fighting Irish had put in 11 unanswered points to jump to a commanding 59–43 lead!

As the final minutes ticked down, SVSM put six more points on their side. Oak Hill, the top-ranked high school team in the country, put only two on theirs. When the buzzer sounded, the final score read SVSM 65, Oak Hill 45.

LeBron's efforts were, undeniably, the biggest reason for that 20-point difference. He had an astonishing 31 points, 13 rebounds, and 6 assists!

Yet LeBron wasn't thinking about his numbers when the game ended. He was celebrating with his teammates and screaming along with the crowd. At one point, he took off the gold band and threw it into the stands for some lucky spectator to catch.

Later, it was time to face the cameras for interviews. LeBron, still breathless from the game and the excitement, nevertheless handled himself well.

"We just wanted to come here today and get a victory," he said in response to a question about his pregame hopes. He acknowledged the pressure that surrounded the game, but also said since he and his teammates gave "one hundred and ten percent" that pressure had vanished once the game began.

The next morning, the sports pages were filled with praise for LeBron. But it was a comment made by Dick Vitale during the broadcast that summed up what most were thinking: "He's the truth, the whole truth, and nothing but the truth."

★ CHAPTER EIGHT ★

2003

Praise and Criticism

LeBron James turned eighteen two and a half weeks after the victory over Oak Hill. Soon after, he got the best birthday present of all: *USA Today* announced its Top 25 High School Teams and SVSM was at the top!

That number-one ranking capped an exciting and media-filled half season for the team, and for LeBron in particular. He'd given interviews, posed for publicity photos, and fielded offers to appear on popular television shows such as *Late Show with David Letterman, CBS Early Show, Good Morning America,* and *Live with Regis and Kelly.* A production company even approached him about appearing in a movie, while a television network wanted him to star in a prime-time show!

The offers were flattering, of course, but they were also distracting, and not just for LeBron. Members of SVSM's administrative staff were forced to handle a constant flow of queries and requests. LeBron's family, friends, classmates, and teammates were also pestered by celebrity hounds seeking the "inside scoop" on LeBron's life.

What such people soon discovered, however, was that off the basketball court, LeBron was much like any typical teenage boy. Schoolwork, hanging out with friends, playing video games — take away the media hype and LeBron seemed like just another kid goofing around with his buddies.

Unfortunately, the media hype was always there, and not always complimentary. In early January, LeBron suffered his first real backlash from the press.

On the first day back at school after the holidays, LeBron drove up in a new car. And not just any car: a platinum-and-black Hummer H2, fully equipped with a state-of-the-art video game system, a DVD player, three televisions, and leather seats and headrests with the words *King James* emblazoned on them. The total cost of the vehicle was estimated at eighty thousand dollars. LeBron said it was an eighteenth birthday present from his mother.

But had the H2 really been a gift purchased for him by Gloria — or had it come from another source, like a shoe company hoping to woo LeBron?

The answer to that question was very important, for if LeBron had accepted a gift from a company hoping to gain favor with him, then, according to state rules, he would have to forfeit his amateur-athlete status.

In other words, he wouldn't be allowed to play the remaining games on SVSM's schedule.

The press took hold of the story and ran with it. *Hummergate!* the headlines screamed. Articles pondered how Gloria, a single mother living in a small apartment in a poor section of Akron, could have possibly secured the necessary loan.

Finally, after two weeks of intrigue, the rumors were laid to rest. Gloria had provided all the necessary paperwork to back up her bank loan claim. True, the H2 was an excessive gift, but it was also legitimate.

The media frenzy died soon after — only to be resurrected when a similar situation came to light. Unfortunately this time, LeBron himself was at the root of the issue.

The problem surrounded two vintage "throwback" sports jerseys he had accepted as gifts from the owner of a Cleveland clothing shop. The price tag on the shirts came to less than nine hundred dollars. But it wasn't the shirts' worth that was at issue, it was that LeBron had given the shop owner autographed photographs in return.

Once again, the high school athletic authorities claimed that LeBron had broken the rules, had given up his amateur status, and therefore, could not finish the season with SVSM.

The owner of the store quickly came to LeBron's defense, saying he'd given LeBron the jerseys as a way of thanking him for being such a good role model to students.

But the appeal fell on deaf ears. On January 31, 2003, LeBron James was benched.

Unbelievably, there were some who said that being sidelined was the best thing for his career. Now he could sign with a shoe company, be free of injury worries, and even enter discussions with NBA teams. What more could he possibly want?

What LeBron wanted was to finish out the season with his best friends and to win another state championship! The endorsements and the NBA would still be there when his high school days were over but the chance to play those last games with Sian, Romeo, Little Dru, and Willie would never come again.

As it turned out, he had that chance after all. Gloria hired a high-powered attorney and after a tense two weeks, the courts issued a new ruling that reinstated him on the team.

LeBron was overjoyed. He was also full of remorse for the trouble he had caused his team. In an interview with former football and baseball star Deion Sanders he said, "There's nothing I'm sorry more about, you know, [than] disrespecting my teammates. . . . I love them to death and I can do nothing without my teammates."

When LeBron returned to the court after the scandal, he came ready to play. The match was against Westchester High School of Los Angeles during the Prime Time Shootout tournament in Trenton, New Jersey. Westchester, number seven in *USA Today*, promised to be tough competition.

LeBron's return was the story before the start of the game. But it was his performance during the game that made headlines the next day. He completely dominated the floor, draining basket after basket after basket. By the end of the game, the Fighting Irish had scored 78 points — 52 of which had been made by LeBron alone, the highest of his career to date!

"I think missing a game last week gave me a little more motivation," he said later, a mischievous smile on his face.

With LeBron back in the lineup, SVSM romped through the rest of their schedule to an 18-1 record. They powered through the playoff season, too, to reach the finals for the fourth time in four years, the only Ohio team ever to do so.

That final game — the last the Fab Five would play together — was against Kettering Alter of Dayton,

Ohio. Earlier in the season, SVSM had bested Kettering 73–40. After such a decisive victory, some believed the Fighting Irish could win with their hands tied behind their backs. But just one year before, SVSM had lost the championship to Roger Bacon, a team they had beaten handily during the regular season. It was just possible that history would repeat itself with this championship.

Not if LeBron had anything to say about it! A mere nineteen seconds into the game, he dodged his defender, snagged a pass down low, and rocketed into air for a monster dunk.

Alter wasn't about to let that kind of play rule this game. They knew that SVSM thrived on fast breaks and lightning-quick action. So they slowed down the game's pace, hoping to thwart SVSM's rhythm. And at first, the strategy worked. By the end of the first half, Alter led 19–14.

But the Irish came back to capture the lead by the end of the third quarter. Seven minutes into the fourth, LeBron tossed in two free throws, a three-pointer, and a corkscrew of a layup for seven points in a row.

Then Alter drew within four in the final minute and narrowly missed a three-pointer that would have tightened the score even more.

In the end, however, when the clock ran out, SVSM had won, 40–36. It was one of the Irish's lowest-scoring games in recent years — and might have been much lower if not for LeBron. He alone accounted for 25 of their points, plus 11 rebounds.

The Fighting Irish went crazy with happiness. "It's all just joy," LeBron said later that night, his now-famous hundred-watt smile lighting his face.

He had every reason to grin. His year-end stats read more like those of a seasoned professional than an eighteen-year-old senior in high school: 31.6 points, 9.6 rebounds, 4.6 assists, and 3.4 steals. Earlier in the season, SVSM had honored him by retiring his jersey number, hanging a replica of it in the school's gym rafters. To make things even better, *USA Today*'s year-end Top 25 list had SVSM still ranked in the number-one slot.

For the senior on the verge of turning pro, that was joy indeed.

★ CHAPTER NINE ★

2003–2004

Onward to the NBA

LeBron James's high school career ended on March 22, 2003, with the victory over Kettering Alter. But he wasn't done playing in high school events, for he had been invited to participate in several postseason games.

First up was McDonald's All American High School Basketball Game in Cleveland. In this week-long show of basketball talent, LeBron won the slam dunk contest and practiced with his teammates before NBA scouts. Later in the week, he opened the East-vs-West game with a tremendous dunk, followed soon after by two free throws, two assists, and a steal — all in the first five minutes! LeBron's team won 122–107 and he was handed the John R. Wooden Award, the tournament's MVP trophy, as recognition for his amazing contribution of 27 points, 7 rebounds, and 7 assists.

Five days later at the EA Sports Roundball Classic in Chicago, he showed amazing grace under pressure. His team, West, was down 119–118 with thirty-one seconds remaining. The opposing team had just been fouled, sending an East player to the free throw line for one-and-one.

The player bounced the ball, shot — missed!

LeBron ripped down the rebound, spun, and dribbled madly down court. A defender gave chase only to see LeBron stop on a dime eight feet from the hoop and toss in a perfect bank shot to win the game. Once again, LeBron received the MVP award.

His final postseason appearance came three weeks later, at the Jordan Capital Classic in Washington, D.C. His team, Black, didn't win that match, but he brought people to their feet by scoring 34 points, making 12 rebounds, and dishing 6 assists. They rose to applaud again when he was given the MVP award — and clapped even harder when he insisted on sharing it with Shannon Brown, whose 27 points and 8 assists for the Silver team had helped them win the game.

Moves like that, and his many on-court, had the NBA breathless with anticipation and hope. The league had been slumping in popularity for several seasons; many believed that it could be saved only by talented, charismatic, and unsullied players such as LeBron James.

On April 25, 2003, LeBron told the public what they'd long hoped to hear. He was going to forego college and enter the NBA Draft. Along with that announcement came his promise to work hard to help his new team, to learn from more experienced players while giving his all, and to face head-on whatever challenges came his way.

Now the question became, which of the thirty NBA teams would get to choose him?

The answer came on May 22, when the draft order was announced. First pick was awarded to the Cleveland Cavaliers, a team that had finished in or near the cellar for several seasons. Although the official draft wouldn't take place until June 26, that the Cavs would choose LeBron James was understood by all, including LeBron.

"I'm staying in Cleveland, and I'm real excited," he said.

He was excited by something else, too. For many months, he had been wooed by Nike, adidas, and Reebok. Now he chose to sign with Nike and in doing so became a millionaire several times over. After years of struggling financially, he and Gloria would never have to worry about money again.

LeBron graduated from SVSM soon after. That day, like so many in his recent past, was bittersweet. He could look back on the last four years with great pride in his accomplishments, both academic and athletic. He was heading toward a great career, but he was also leaving behind teachers and staff who had stood by him throughout his rise to fame, and a team and coaches that had fostered his talent and helped him become the player he was.

And he was leaving behind his best friends, the people he cherished most in his life after Gloria — people who, by his own admission, kept him real because they knew him so well. In fact, when someone once asked him how he would handle the pressures of fame and fortune, he replied, "I've got nothing to worry about. I've got my friends to keep me cool. I've got this inner circle. As long as you've got friends, you've got nothing to worry about."

Nothing, that is, except disappointing his new teammates, his fans, and the NBA. No one doubted for a minute that LeBron had great talent, but what no one knew, including LeBron, was how he would perform with and against professionals who had been playing in the big leagues for years. Would he shine like the bright light everyone believed him to be — or would he flame out, as so many other brilliant prospects had before him?

His play during the Cavs summer league didn't give a definite answer to that question. During some games he dazzled with his variety of no-look passes, thunderous dunks, and heads-up play. Other times, he seemed more tentative and unsure, muffing easy lay-ups and clanging jump shots off the rim. But those games were merely a warm-up for his official NBA debut.

★ CHAPTER TEN ★

2003–2004

"The Real Deal"

According to the Sacramento Kings media office, more than double the number of press passes than normal were issued on October 29, 2003. That's because the Cleveland Cavaliers were in town to play their first game of the season. But the press wasn't coming to see the Kings and Cavs battle on the court — they were there to see LeBron James's official professional debut.

They would not go home disappointed.

Although the Cavs lost to the Kings 106–92, LeBron was magnificent. Nine minutes into the game, he had scored ten points including three-for-three jump shots from the baseline!

Then, with less than two minutes remaining in the first quarter, he swiped the ball from Sacramento's Mike Bibby and sent it to teammate Carlos Boozer. Boozer converted the pass into a dunk. Two points for the Cavs, one steal and one assist for LeBron.

Moments later, LeBron stole the ball again. With all

cameras focused on him, he ran the length of the court and slammed down a massive tomahawk dunk. Photographs of that shot would appear on posters and blogs almost overnight and it remains one of his signature moments.

But as his former SVSM teammates knew and his new teammates were discovering, LeBron wasn't all about showboating. Less than a minute after his slam, he stole the ball again. The way to the hoop was clear. But instead of running and slamming again, LeBron held the ball for a moment and then shoveled it to teammate Ricky Davis who thumped in the dunk for two.

Those selfless, heads-up plays brought the spectators to their feet. LeBron's game stats of 25 points, 9 assists, 6 rebounds, and 4 steals were the highest of any prep-to-pro player ever; compared to other greats, his 25 points were nine more than Michael Jordan had made in his debut game, and just one less than Magic Johnson. The numbers made the Cavs' front office smile broadly and members of press nod knowingly as they wrote their stories. The hype about this youngster wasn't wrong: LeBron James was, as one Sacramento King put it, "the real deal."

LeBron himself seemed to have mixed emotions about his performance. "Running up and down with NBA players, it's a dream," he said before adding, "I think I could have helped my team a little bit more down the stretch, I could have been a little bit more aggressive to help us get the win."

Unfortunately, getting a win wouldn't happen right away for the Cavs. They played four more games, all losses, before finally chalking up their first victory in early November. They won again the next night, too, but by the end of the month had added only two more while giving up thirteen. Some of the matches had been lost by only a few points but others had had wider gaps. LeBron had played well for the most part, but there was no way he could single-handedly turn around a team that had won only seventeen games the previous season.

He didn't stop trying, however. On his nineteenth birthday, he played his thirty-second professional game. Of those thirty-two, he had reached double digits in scoring in all but five. He also had six double-double games and once, in mid-December, nearly reached triple-double numbers with 32 points, 10 rebounds, and 9 assists.

Unfortunately, his birthday also saw the Cavs lose their twenty-second game.

LeBron tried not to let the losses get him down. Instead, after the New Year, he worked even harder to make every point, every steal, every assist, and every rebound add up to a win. And the team's record did improve. Following the All-Star break in mid-

February — an event that saw LeBron leading the charge in the Rookie Challenge against a team of players in their second season — they had a seven-game winning streak that brought their record to 31–36. Sadly, the streak was followed by four losses. But at least the wins had given Cleveland fans reason to hope that things might turn around.

Soon after that fourth loss, LeBron gave them even more reason to hope.

On March 27, 2004, the Cavs faced the New Jersey Nets on their home court. The game started out as usual for Cleveland — that is, they were losing at the end of the first quarter. So far, LeBron had been dismal, hitting only a single bucket in four attempts.

But midway through the second quarter, LeBron woke up. During a four-and-a-half minute segment, he tossed in eleven straight points to put the Cavs up 40–35.

Unfortunately, New Jersey's Lucious Harris was just as hot-handed. He went six-for-six in the second to give the Nets the lead, 52–44, at halftime. In the third quarter, that eight-point lead grew to eleven. The Cavs closed the gap again, but were still down by three going into the fourth.

After Cleveland's four recent losses, few people expected the Cavs to win. They were wrong.

In the middle of the fourth, Cleveland exploded. They outscored the Nets 10–3 to tie it all up 96–96 with less than four minutes remaining. The tying shot had come on a pass from LeBron. One free throw later, the Cavs had a single-point lead over the Nets.

Then, as the clock passed the two-minute mark, LeBron went on a scoring rampage. First he made a nineteen-foot jumper. Two points. Then two free throws. Four. Then, amazingly, in the last forty seconds he drove to the hoop three times for three more buckets — six, eight, *ten!* The last of these, a two-handed slam, sealed the game for the Cavs, 107–104.

Those ten points brought LeBron's game total to a career high of 41, making him the youngest rookie in NBA history to score 40 or more in a single game. He also had a career high of 13 assists, plus 6 rebounds and 3 steals, proving once more that for LeBron James, it was team first, self second.

LeBron's amazing rookie season ended less than a month later. His year-end averages of 20.9 points, 5.5 rebounds, 5.9 assists, and 1.6 steals per game were as strong as Michael Jordan's had been in his rookie year. He had led his team in scoring, steals, minutes, earned 12 double-doubles, made 30 or more points in 13 games, and been the youngest player in NBA history to reach the one thousand point milestone.

But LeBron's contribution to the team went far beyond his own numbers. Thanks to his efforts, the Cavs finished with a record of 35 wins, 47 losses, a definite improvement over their previous 17-65 year. They narrowly missed taking a spot in the playoffs.

"That was my main concern — that we get better from day one," he said.

To no one's surprise, LeBron was voted to receive the NBA's prestigious Rookie of the Year award, the youngest player ever to receive that honor. At the ceremony, he thanked his teammates, his coaches, and the league for their support and trust. But before them all came someone even more important:

"I would like to thank my mother," he said in his acceptance speech. "She's been there from day one."

Paul Silas, the Cavaliers' coach, fully recognized what LeBron had done for the team. "Whatever was needed, he provided for us."

Another admiring coach summed up LeBron with one simple rhetorical question: "How are you going to stop *him*?"

★ CHAPTER ELEVEN ★

2004–2005

No Slumping Sophomore

With his rookie season behind him, LeBron James removed his Cavaliers jersey to don a navy blue and red one with the letters USA emblazoned on the front. It was an Olympic year and LeBron was headed to Athens for the competition in August. He was the youngest player ever to suit up for Team USA and was excited for the opportunity.

"It's a dream come true for me to represent my country," he told reporters.

Unfortunately, that dream fell short of a gold medal. Despite a roster of massive talent, Team USA walked away with a bronze. Some observers felt the reason for the third-place showing was because the team was made up of superstars who all wanted to take top billing.

But others grumbled that the loss was Coach Larry Brown's fault. They said he should have played LeBron more since the team played better when he was on the floor. Overall, LeBron played an average of 12.1 minutes over eight games, and logged 5.4 points, 1.0 rebounds, and 1.6 assists in that time.

LeBron, while disappointed with the team's showing, didn't criticize his coach or dwell on the loss. He was too busy preparing for his sophomore season with the Cavaliers — and for the media onslaught that would come with it.

He was also preparing for something that some nineteen-year-old men might find intimidating: fatherhood. Eight days before LeBron's first preseason game, his longtime girlfriend, Savannah Brinson, gave birth to their son, LeBron James Junior.

"This is a happy time for me," the new father told reporters. But beyond that, he chose to keep the matter private and to focus on basketball.

The Cavaliers won six of eight games in the October preseason. But they seemed to fall apart at first when the official season began, losing an overtime opening match to the Indiana Pacers and then dropping two more in the first week. Some said they were adjusting to the departure of one of their key players, Carlos Boozer, who now played for the Utah Jazz.

If so, they adjusted quickly in the next weeks. One victory followed another, until they had racked up 9 wins in their next 11 games to end November with a record of 9-5.

One of those wins came on November 24 against the Detroit Pistons. That night, LeBron showed that while other second-year players might suffer from the so-called "sophomore slump," he wouldn't. In the first quarter, he brought fans to their feet with a slam dunk less than three minutes in. Two minutes later, he threw down another. By the end of the first 12 minutes, he had chalked up 14 of Cleveland's 24 points. He added 7 more in the second quarter to help his team to a 54–37 lead going into halftime.

But the Pistons weren't ready to throw in the towel just yet. They exploded in the first minutes of the second half, scoring eight straight points.

LeBron didn't let them steal the game, however. At 9:07, he dished an assist to teammate Eric Snow who stuck an eighteen-foot jump shot to put the Cavs back up by ten. Then, at 8:26, he drained in a three-pointer from twenty-five feet out. Less than thirty seconds later, he did it again, sticking out his tongue and nodding with glee as the ball swished through the hoop.

The Cavs bulldozed their way to a 92–76 win. LeBron accounted for 43 of those points, the most made by any player so far that season. He also had 6 rebounds and 5 assists.

"We just don't have enough superlatives to give this guy," Coach Silas said later.

LeBron continued to top the ranks of high scorers

in the games leading up to the All-Star break. Out of 24 played, there was only one game in which he scored less than 20 points; his usual tally was closer to 30. Midway through January, LeBron posted his fourth double-double of the season — and followed up that performance the next night by becoming the youngest player in NBA history to record a triple-double.

Behind his masterful 27-point, 11-rebound, 10-assist effort that night, the Cavs jumped to a record of 23–14, one of their best in years. As was typical, LeBron was pleased with his triple-double, but even happier that his team had won. "Individual aspects mean nothing to me," he said. "I'm a team player. I just want to see our team winning games."

Unfortunately, soon after the All-Star Game in February — LeBron's first — the Cavs went into a slump, losing six games in a row, then winning three, only to lose two more.

Some players might have slumped, too, in such a situation. But not LeBron. After that second straight loss, he raised his game to a nearly unimaginable height.

The Cavaliers traveled to Toronto on March 20, 2005, to face the Raptors. Eight minutes into the game, the Raptors had a 12-point lead.

Cleveland fans sighed. Were the Cavs destined for yet another loss?

Not if LeBron James had anything to say about it. He already had eight points, and at 3:36 on the clock, he added two more with a jump shot to make the score 23–13 Raptors. He doubled his point total by the end of the quarter with five free throws and a buzzer-beating three-pointer. With those shots, the Cavs drew to within three of the Raptors.

But still, Cleveland couldn't seem to push ahead. They trailed throughout the second quarter and into the third, sometimes by as many as seven points.

Then one minute into the second half, Cleveland closed the gap to one when Zydrunas Ilgauskas was fouled while making a layup.

The score remained 57–56 for nearly two minutes. Then Raptor Morris Peterson ripped down a defensive rebound and tried to pass to a teammate. The ball never made it to the intended player, however, because LeBron stole it — and then converted the steal into a three-point play to give the Cavs their first lead, 59–57!

That bucket brought his game total to 32 points. With nearly twenty minutes left to play, people began to take notice. LeBron had played 40-points-or-more games before, but might this be the night he reached 50?

Perhaps. By the end of the third quarter, he had 38. In the fourth, he continued to drain shot after shot, including a booming dunk punctuated by a rebel yell that was shown on sports highlights over and over. Then, with 2:22 showing on the clock, he put in one more to score his 49th and 50th points of the game!

But he wasn't through yet. The Cavs were down by 99–92. As the last minutes ticked down, LeBron stuck a three-pointer. 99–95.

The Raptors answered with two of their own. 101–95.

Cleveland's Drew Gooden tried for a three-point shot. He missed. Teammate Ira Newble crashed the boards and came down with the rebound. He got the ball to LeBron. LeBron shot from twenty-five feet out. Made it!

Still, the Raptors had the lead, 103–98. Could the Cavaliers surge ahead in the final thirty seconds?

They couldn't. Instead, Toronto boosted their lead by four to take the game 107–98.

LeBron was sorely disappointed. Sure, with 56 points, he had just become the youngest player in the NBA to score more than 50 points in a single game. But that wasn't what mattered to him.

"I played well, probably the best game of my life," he said, "but it means nothing when you come away with a loss."

Earlier in the season, a spot in the playoffs had seemed certain for the Cavs. Now, with their record at 34–30, that spot was slowly slipping from their grasp.

On April 20, it disappeared altogether when the New Jersey Nets beat the Boston Celtics to claim the eighth berth.

LeBron had done all he could to help his team. His end-of-season stats were absolutely phenomenal for a second-year player. His 27.2 points, 7.4 rebounds, and 7.2 assists made him one of only five players in NBA history to average 27, 7, and 7. The others were Oscar Robertson, John Havlicek, Larry Bird, and Michael Jordan. He'd also posted four triple-doubles, scored 30 or more points in 27 games, and 40 or more in 5.

That it all went to waste was no doubt frustrating for the twenty-year-old. Still, he tried to put things into perspective.

"This is just basketball," he said after the game. "I do this because I love to do this, but I got family members at home. That is what is most important."

CHAPTER TWELVE

2005–2006

Playoff Potential

LeBron James had been a professional basketball player for two years. In his rookie season, he had lofted the Cavaliers record from 17–65 to 35–47. Attendance at home games jumped from approximately 11,500 to 18,250. The next year, it had grown to 19,000 as the Cavs soared to a record of 42–40 behind LeBron.

LeBron's popularity soared, too, as the huge sales of his Nike shoes and Cavalier jerseys with his name and number proved. But he wasn't just popular among fans; comments made by his teammates, opponents, coaches, and sportswriters showed he was well-liked by his peers, too. These people, most of whom had been in or around the league for many years, considered LeBron to be one of the most mature, intelligent, and charismatic players in the game. He was also one of the least selfish — in short, a leader.

LeBron accepted that role with his typical grace. And as a leader, he had one important goal: to make it to the NBA championships. He was determined to reach that goal in his third season.

The Cavaliers' front office was equally determined. They made some significant changes, the first of which was to replace coach Paul Silas with rookie coach Mike Brown. Veteran players Donyell Marshall, Larry Hughes, and Damon Jones were added to the lineup; Zydrunas Ilgauskas's contract was renewed. With LeBron at the helm, the Cavaliers went into the 2005–2006 season looking stronger and feeling more confident than ever before.

After a strong 5–3 preseason, the Cavaliers opened the regular schedule on November 2 with a home game against the New Orleans Hornets. More than 20,000 spectators packed into the arena. They all were looking forward to a night of outstanding basketball with LeBron James as the star of the show. They did not leave disappointed.

The Cavaliers' offense exploded for 35 points in the first quarter, nearly double the points made by the Hornets. LeBron accounted for 12 of those points, including a beautiful three-pointer with thirty-nine seconds left on the clock.

LeBron took a rest early in the second quarter but three minutes after reentering the game, he put on a shooting demonstration.

Zip! He stole the ball from Bostjan Nachbar and

then *bam!* lobbed a three-pointer from twenty-five feet out on the right. Less than thirty seconds later *bam!* he drained another three-point shot from the left. Thirty seconds after that *bam!* he poured an-other one in from the top of the key.

Fweet! New Orleans called a time-out, hoping to stop the onslaught.

It didn't work. Fifteen seconds after the two teams resumed play, LeBron hit yet another three-pointer, bringing his two-minute total to four shots for 12 points!

The spectators were in awe. So were the players. "We were just like the fans," Donyell Marshall said. "We wanted him to keep shooting, too."

LeBron did keep shooting, adding another three-pointer for five in a row, six for the night. After that last one, he amused the fans by blowing on his finger-tips as if to cool his hot hand. Not surprisingly, the Cavaliers won easily, 109–87.

Unfortunately, two nights later the Cavaliers found themselves on the wrong side of a similarly lopsided score. The San Antonio Spurs' defense zeroed in on LeBron and held him to a mere ten points in the last three quarters to take the game, 102–76.

However, that loss turned out to be the exception rather than the rule for the Cavaliers that month. On

November 13, they beat the Orlando Magic 108–100 in overtime, their fourth straight victory.

That same night, LeBron entered the game just ten shy of becoming the youngest player to reach 4,000 career points. He made two of the ten early on with a jump shot. Then he drove in for layup for two more and did the same again minutes later to bring his total to six. His next two points came thanks to a monster dunk. Then, before a crowd of fans screaming his name, he swished the ball through the hoop from twenty-one feet away a minute before the end of the first quarter, racking up points 3,999 and 4,000!

LeBron knew he had just broken a record but he didn't stop to celebrate. There was a game on the line and he intended to win. But as the clock ticked down, it looked as if the Magic would emerge victorious, for they were up 88–85 with only 18.1 seconds remaining.

Then suddenly, *swish!* A Cavalier made a three-pointer to tie things up as the buzzer sounded! For once, the hero of the game wasn't LeBron James, but his new teammate Donyell Marshall.

The Cavs won four more after that overtime victory but their streak ended at eight when they lost to the Pacers at the end of November. During that time, LeBron racked up the stats, including a double-double and three 30-plus-point games.

The Cavs were 10–4 going into the second month of the season. On December 10, they traveled to Milwaukee to face the Bucks. The two teams had nearly identical records and fans looked forward to a fierce battle. They got that and, thanks to LeBron, much more.

The Bucks drew first blood but the Cavs answered quickly with two free throws from Ilgauskas and a jump shot from LeBron. Three minutes into the game Cleveland had inched ahead. They kept the lead throughout the first half and into the second.

Then, four minutes into the third quarter, the Bucks jumped up by one. The Cavs worked to regain their lead — and none so hard as LeBron James. Jump shots from twenty feet out. Driving layups through tight defense. Arcing three-pointers over waving arms. Pressure-packed free throws. Again and again, he hit his target, passing the 30-, 40-, and 50-point marks on his way to a total of 52.

But his efforts were for naught. After tying the score at 98–98 with four minutes remaining, the Cavs slipped behind for good and eventually lost 106–111.

LeBron tried to make light of the loss and to downplay the fact that he had single-handedly scored nearly half his team's points. "I don't want to score 50 again for the rest of my career because I am now 0–2 when I score 50," he said. "I don't look at it as me playing well. It's the fact that we didn't get a win and that's all I care for."

One month later, however, LeBron did score over 50 again — and this time, his team won.

In fact, winning was something the Cavaliers were doing a lot of that season. LeBron's consistently superior play was a huge part of their success, but thanks to strong performances by his teammates, he was no longer carrying the entire team on his broad shoulders. And that, it seemed, made a world of difference to the team's record.

At the start of the season, LeBron had predicted that the Cavs could be a 50-win team that year. With a final, nail-biting 100–99 victory over the Atlanta Hawks on April 19, 2006 — a game he sat out due to a sprained ankle — his prediction came true. The Cavs ended the regular season with a record of 50–32; three days later, they made their first appearance in the playoffs since 1993.

That night, all eyes were on LeBron James as he took to the court for his postseason debut game. Everyone knew how good he had been in the regular season, for with 31.4 points, 7.0 rebounds, and 6.6 assists he was one of only four players in league history to achieve 31–7–6 in a season.

Yet some worried that he would crack under the

pressure of the playoffs. After all, plenty of more experienced players had reached this point in the past only to falter.

Not LeBron. That first game, he dominated in every category, pure and simple. He shot from outside, inside, and downtown. He dished, flipped, and rocketed the ball into his teammates' waiting hands. He ripped down rebounds from both hoops. By the game's end, a 97–86 win over the Washington Wizards, he had double digits in points (32), rebounds (11), and assists (11). That triple-double was the first made in the playoffs since Magic Johnson had done the same in 1980.

"It's a great class to be in," LeBron said with a huge grin later that night.

Unfortunately for Cleveland fans, Washington evened up the series three nights later. But in Game 3, it was a different story with a thrilling ending that featured LeBron as the main character.

Washington took the lead early on and held it throughout the first half, sometimes by as much as twelve points. But in the third quarter, Cleveland slowly closed the gap and then finally erased it altogether by tying it 71–71 going into the fourth. The Wizards inched ahead again in the first minutes only to find the Cavaliers putting the pedal to the metal and catching up yet again.

With fifty seconds left on the clock, the score was

knotted at 93 each. Twenty seconds later, LeBron got his hands on the ball and rolled in a layup to put his team ahead by two. That lead lasted all of seven seconds, when Gilbert Arenas, Washington's star player, drove in for a layup. The ball went in — and Arenas was fouled by LeBron! One free throw later, the Wizards were up by one.

There were less than twenty seconds left in the game. The Cavaliers knew what they had to do to win. They had to get the ball to LeBron.

Tick. Tick. Tick. The seconds counted down from twenty to fifteen. To ten. To seven. To six.

Then it happened. LeBron got the ball. He drove toward the hoop, shoved his way past one Wizard, and knocked into another. Four feet from the basket, he jumped and shot. The ball soared over the defense's grasping hands, kissed the glass, and banked in! Two points — and victory!

"I said I wouldn't have two bad games in a row," LeBron said, referring the previous loss, when he had 10 turnovers and shot 7-for-25.

Two nights later, the Wizards took Game 4 to tie the series at two games each. In Game 5, the two teams paced each other point for point throughout most of the match. Then, in the fourth quarter, the Cavaliers took the lead — only to see it dissolve in the final minutes to send the game into overtime.

Tension mounted as the teams traded the lead and the minutes ticked down to seconds. Then Arenas tied it up, 119–119, with a free throw with only three seconds left, and bumped the Wizards up by one on his second throw from the line. It seemed that Washington would emerge victorious.

Unbelievably, they didn't because of a play that would later be called "The Layup."

With three seconds remaining, Larry Hughes inbounded the ball to LeBron. LeBron danced free of Antawn Jamison, shimmied a few feet just inside the baseline, dodged a Washington triple-team defense, and, with .9 showing on the shot clock, leaped up to roll the ball off his long fingertips into the hoop.

The crowd went insane. So did the Cavaliers. Crack under pressure? Hardly! LeBron had saved the game again!

"If I wore an eighteen- or nineteen-size shoe, I wouldn't have made it," he joked later. "But I wear a sixteen and was able to tightrope that baseline to get a layup."

The Cavs were up 3–2 in the series. Two nights later, they beat the Wizards to move to the semifinals. There, they faced the Detroit Pistons, a team renowned for its defense. That defense went to work the minute Cleveland hit the court and didn't let up until they'd routed the Cavaliers from the series, four games to three. A

big part of their strategy was to triple-team LeBron —
and it worked, especially in the final loss where he
scored just one bucket in the second half.

But even the Pistons couldn't stop Cleveland's top
player completely. He posted two triple-doubles in the
series and narrowly missed a third. As always, however,
his personal stats meant nothing to LeBron when his
team lost. And as always, he did his best to learn from
his mistakes and look toward the future goal. For him,
that goal remained straightforward: "Win the championship. Simple as that."

✶ CHAPTER THIRTEEN ✶

2006–2007

Road to the Finals

The months after the postseason were busy for Le-
Bron. He spent time with his mother, his girlfriend,
and his young son. He dispelled rumors that he was
going to another team by signing a new four-year contract with Cleveland. And in mid-August, he played
for Team USA in the FIBA (Fédération Internationale
de Basketball, or International Basketball Federation)
World's Championship in Japan.

In the past, the United States basketball program
had been the most dominant in the world. But now
other countries were equal to, and in some cases better
than, America's team. That was proven when Spain
took the gold medal and Greece the silver, leaving the
USA with the bronze.

Back in the United States, it was time to prepare for
the NBA season — and the ultimate goal of winning
the championship. To achieve that goal, Cavalier coach
Mike Brown chose to limit LeBron's preseason minutes

so that he'd be fully rested for the games that counted. Of the seven games, he sat out two, came off the bench for one, and played less than forty-eight minutes in the other four. Six of those seven games were Cavalier losses, unfortunately.

Still, what happens in the preseason isn't always an indication of what a team can do. Cleveland opened with a hard-fought win over the Washington Wizards. They added another victory two nights later, beating the San Antonio Spurs 88–81. It was the first time since 1988 that the Cavs had bested the Spurs in San Antonio. That night also saw LeBron James posting his first double-double of the season.

Those two wins were followed by two losses but then Cleveland went on a five-game tear. They ended the first month with a solid record of nine wins, six losses.

December found the Cavaliers seesawing back and forth, winning one night, losing the next. LeBron continued to play well, although not for as many minutes as he had the previous year. Still, in the minutes he played he racked up the points, including a game one week before his twenty-second birthday, when he made his seven thousandth career point.

"James may have to have his name legally changed to 'LeBron James, the youngest player ever' as it seems that he hits these kind of milestones on a regular basis," one sportswriter joked.

One month later, he ruled the courts again. That night, January 24, the Cavaliers played the Philadelphia 76ers. A close game throughout, the match went into overtime after the Sixers sank a buzzer-beating jump shot. It went into a second overtime thanks to two free throws by LeBron. Those shots gave James 26 points for the night — with more to come.

In the five minutes of the second overtime, LeBron scored an astonishing thirteen points, nine of them on three-pointers! But in the end, his efforts were for nothing. The Cavs lost, 118–115.

LeBron and his teammates were bitterly disappointed with the loss. "When a team comes in here and beats you on your home court, that's deflating," James said. "We have to get a win."

They did win the next game, but then fell back into the pattern of winning a few, losing a few. Fortunately, they wound up winning more than they lost, even when LeBron was forced to the sidelines with an injured toe at the end of January. By the end of February, their record stood at 33–24, putting them on pace for another 50-game season.

Then came March, when most basketball followers turn away from the NBA to watch the best college teams battle for supremacy in March Madness. But this year, many eyes stayed glued to the Cavaliers, for LeBron and his teammates were busy driving their fans crazy — crazy with joy, that is. After dropping the first game, Cleveland stormed the courts and won eight in a row!

LeBron, as always, played an enormous part in those victories. He reached double digits in points, rebounds, and assists in several outings. On March 7, he shot a season-high of 41 points. A week later, he broke yet another NBA "youngest ever" record when he made his eight thousandth career point. Three nights after that, he had his best rebounding effort of the season with seventeen. At month's end, he preserved his team's second-place ranking with a seven-point overtime effort for Cleveland's eleventh win in four weeks. Nine games later, the Cavaliers ended their regular season with a record of 50 wins, 32 losses.

LeBron's stats of 27.3 points, 6.7 rebounds and 6.0 assists weren't as strong as they'd been the year before, but then again, he hadn't played as many minutes as in 2005–2006 either. And his numbers were still good enough to put him in the record books alongside Oscar Robertson, the only other player to average 27–6–6 three years in a row.

Of course, LeBron wasn't that interested in his numbers. He had bigger things on his mind after all, chiefly, winning the NBA Championship. To do that, he and the Cavaliers first had to beat three other teams.

★ CHAPTER FOURTEEN ★

2007

A Champion Without a Championship

The Cavaliers' first opponents in the 2007 playoffs were the Washington Wizards. Four games later, the Wizards were down and out, having been swept clean out of contention by LeBron and his teammates.

The New Jersey Nets proved more difficult to beat. After going up 2–0 in the series, the Cavs dropped the third game. They won the next night, however, but once more saw their two-game lead drop to one the following game.

Then came Game 6. By halftime, Cleveland was up 53–38 and looked to have the series in the bag. But the Nets didn't give up. They chipped away at the Cavs' lead, something that became easier when LeBron was forced to the bench after making his fourth personal foul five minutes into the third quarter. When that quarter ended, the score was Cleveland 61, Nets 60!

LeBron wasn't about to let the game slip through his

fingers. He got back in at the start of the fourth and proceeded to contribute 9 points and 3 assists that added 9 more. Behind his drive, Cleveland surged ahead to take the game, 88–72.

LeBron was exhausted but exhilarated after the victory. "It's a great feeling," he said. "This is one of the best feelings I've ever had as a basketball player."

Next up in the playoffs were the always powerful Pistons. LeBron and the Cavaliers hadn't forgotten the sting of losing to Detroit in the semifinals the year before. They wanted nothing more than to trounce their mid-Atlantic rivals.

But at first, it seemed they would not be granted that wish. The Pistons won the first two games by duplicate scores of 79–76.

The Cavaliers were not to be denied, however. They took Game 3 and Game 4 to knot the series at two apiece.

The tiebreaking game was played before a raucous crowd in Detroit. The Pistons had a six-point lead going into the second quarter but the Cavaliers muscled their way back to draw within one at halftime. Midway into the third, Detroit jumped ahead again 65–58 — only to see Cleveland tie it up 70–70 on a last-second three-pointer made by rookie Daniel Gibson on an assist from LeBron.

LeBron sat out the first few minutes of the fourth.

The rest must have been just what he needed, for when he reentered the game, he was on fire. He quickly added 2 points to the 19 he'd already made. Those 21 points became 23 after a driving layup. Less than a minute later, he stuck a three-pointer.

Those seven points helped the Cavs come within one. But to win the game, they needed more — and time was running out.

Thirty seconds remained on the clock when *boom!* LeBron got his hands on the ball and slammed down a thunderous dunk. Cleveland was ahead 89–88!

But before Cavalier fans could even begin to cheer, that lead vanished when Piston sharpshooter Chauncey Billups drained a three-pointer. 91–89 Detroit. The home team would win if they could hang onto that lead for just another twenty seconds.

They couldn't — LeBron James saw to that. With less than a second left on the shot clock, he gathered up the ball, steamed past the defense like a powerful locomotive, jumped up, and threw down *another* dunk an instant before the buzzer sounded! Tie game!

As the fans went wild, the Cavaliers and the Pistons returned to the court for overtime play. LeBron was fouled in the first seconds. He made two from the line. Cavs 93, Pistons 91.

Ten seconds later, Detroit put in two free throws,

then added two more on a jump shot. 95–93 in favor of the Pistons.

LeBron answered with yet another dunk one and a half minutes into play. Tie game again. And then he scored again — and again, and again, and again. Every time a Piston player made a shot to give Detroit the lead, LeBron took that lead away from them. When the five-minute overtime ended, the score was still tied, 100–100. Amazingly, LeBron had made all of Cleveland's overtime points!

The second overtime began much as the first had, with LeBron chalking up two points for the lead and Detroit tying it with two of their own. Then, as the clock ticked past the two-minute mark, the Pistons took a three-point lead.

Cleveland fans held their breath. Would they be able to meet and beat that lead?

The answer wasn't quick in coming, but when it came, it came with a vengeance and at the hands of one of the league's most masterful players, LeBron James. With little more than a minute remaining, he lofted a shot from behind the three-point line. Up, up, up — and in! Tie game again!

The tension mounted as the seconds clicked by. Who would score first — or would neither team score, forcing an unprecedented third overtime?

At :53, Piston Richard Hamilton threatened with a jump shot. Missed.

Anderson Varejao attempted a layup for the Cavaliers with thirty seconds left. Missed.

Detroit's Rasheed Wallace got hold of the ball, popped up for a jumper. Blocked by Varejao and captured by Donyell Marshall with thirteen seconds showing on the clock.

Cleveland called a time-out. When play resumed, everyone in the arena knew the Cavs would try to get the ball to LeBron — and then pray that he could get a shot off before the final eleven seconds elapsed.

What happened next was one of the most pivotal moments in LeBron James's career. He got the ball at midcourt and put it to the floor. One dribble, two, three, and he was in the midst of the Pistons, the most feared defense in the league. Yet those players seemed to be standing still compared to LeBron, who was, quite simply, poetry in motion.

He leaped, pumping the ball from high to low as if to protect it with his body. Then, as he reached the apex of his jump, legs wide, he whipped the ball up again and banked it ever-so-softly against the glass.

Swish — LeBron had just won the game for his team, and with two seconds to spare!

Later, in the Cavaliers' locker room, someone relayed

an astonishing statistic to coach Mike Brown. LeBron James, who had 48 points for the night, had single-handedly made Cleveland's final 25 points — and 29 of their final 30!

LeBron was elated, of course, but he had other feelings after the game as well.

"I'm banged up. I'm winded. I'm fatigued," he admitted in a press conference immediately after the win. But then he cracked a small smile and added, "It's going to be tough to get some rest when [I've] got a crazy two-year-old running around the house. So hopefully, I can take him to one of his grandma's houses."

Whatever rest he and the other Cavaliers got paid off. After fighting for a one-point lead at the end of the third quarter, they pounded the Pistons in the last to win 98–82 and their first-ever shot at the Championship Title.

"This is probably the best feeling that I've ever had in my life," LeBron said that night as he walked around with a dazed but delighted smile on his face.

Unfortunately, that feeling wouldn't last. Five days after beating the Pistons, Cleveland fell to the mighty San Antonio Spurs, 85–76, in Game 1 of the NBA Finals. Game 2 found them losing again, this time 103 to 92. The score of Game 3 was much closer and might have gone into overtime had LeBron's three-point shot at the buzzer dropped in. But it didn't and the Cavaliers suddenly found themselves three games in the hole.

One night later, LeBron became a father for the second time when Savannah gave birth to another son, Bryce Maximus James. That would prove to be the high point of his week, for the next evening, his dream of winning the championship ended with a heartbreaking 83–82 loss. The Spurs were the champs; the Cavs were second-best. In the press conference that followed the championship, LeBron James slumped over the desk and answered each question in a low voice filled with disappointment. That he blamed himself for the loss became clearer with his every sentence.

"I could've been better," he told the media. "I've got a lot of things to work on . . . not just one thing . . . it's everything. I need to definitely get better."

★ CHAPTER FIFTEEN ★

2007–2008

Better . . . But Not Yet Best

LeBron James may have left the Championships believing he needed to improve, but his team and his fans would have argued otherwise. One only has to remember that in four short seasons, he's helped the Cavs jump from a 17-35 record to their first appearance in the finals.

LeBron James's top priority during the 2007 off-season was following through on his promise to himself, his teammates, and his fans to improve his game in any way he could. But those months weren't all about basketball. In mid-July, he co-hosted the ESPY (Excellence in Sports Performance Yearly) awards with comedian Jimmy Kimmel. On September 29, he had a chance to show off his own comedic talents as host of *Saturday Night Live*. He also had laser surgery on his eyes to improve his vision.

The NBA preseason began in early October. This year, the league had arranged for several teams to play games in other parts of the world. The Cavs were scheduled to play two of their seven preseason matches in China. Both were against the Orlando Magic. Both ended in Cleveland losses, as did four of their other games. Their sole victory, a 96–90 overtime battle against the Detroit Pistons, saw LeBron scoring 17 points and contributing 4 assists and 4 rebounds in 25 minutes of play.

Their regular season opened with a game against the Dallas Mavericks on Halloween night. LeBron amused the audience before the game by appearing in a business suit that duplicated his look on one of his new Nike commercials.

But unfortunately, he failed to entertain during the game itself — just the opposite, in fact, for in the first half, he didn't make a single basket! Then, in the second, he tossed in just two buckets in eleven attempts. During those same minutes, he committed five turnovers. In all, he added just ten points to the score. With their star offensive player so off his mark, the Cavs lost 92–74.

It wasn't a strong beginning for the team that had made it to the finals the prior season. But in the very next game, against the New York Knicks, LeBron showed his fans that he was still a scoring powerhouse by draining 45 points — the 18th time in his career that he had a 40+ point game. He also ripped down a team best of 7 rebounds and dished 7 assists, three of which helped his teammate, Daniel Gibson, toss in four 3-pointers.

"That's the thing about LeBron that everybody loves," Gibson said after the 110–106 victory. "He had 45 but he's still finding his teammates and getting everybody involved."

James continued to rack up the stats in the following weeks. He crashed the boards in two games, pulling down 13 total rebounds one night, and 15 the night after that. That second game saw him with his first triple-double of the season, posting 32 points and 13 assists in addition to his double digit rebounding effort.

His last points of that game were classic James: a 24-foot three-pointer that tied the score at 101–101 with just six seconds left to go. A shot at victory in overtime seemed inevitable. But then Devon Williams of the Utah Jazz snared the inbound toss and drove in for a last-second layup to give his team the win.

James was undoubtedly disappointed with the loss, but as always, put it behind him to focus on the games ahead. And with that focus, he helped the Cavs to seven victories out of their next eleven matches. Ten of those games saw him scoring no fewer than 22 points; three of them were triple-double efforts.

That LeBron only posted 15 points in the eleventh was not due to a poor performance, but an injury. As he went up for a shot, the player guarding him batted the ball out of his hands. The block wrenched Le-Bron's left index finger, spraining it badly enough to bench him for the rest of the game, as well as the next five matches.

Just how much of a presence LeBron was on the court became obvious in those games. While the other Cavs did their best to pick up the slack, they lost all five matches, three by more than ten points. James returned in mid-December, coming off the bench for the only time in his 333 games. He made an impact the moment he hit the court, sparking the Cavs to a 118–105 win over the Indiana Pacers.

When asked after the game how it felt not to start, James smiled and replied, "That was one and done for me. I will not be coming off the bench anymore!"

Yet even with LeBron back in the lineup, the Cavs were not winning regularly. On December 29, one day before James's twenty-third birthday, they played their 31st game of the season — and posted their 17th loss. Critics started whispering that Cleveland might not make it to the playoffs again that year.

But those critics were silenced the next month. The Cavs went on a tear, winning eleven games and dropping only three to turn their record from 14–17 to 25–

20! LeBron James was a huge part of that success. He was nearly unstoppable from the floor, draining bucket after bucket night after night. One game he chalked up 51 points, the fourth 50-plus effort of his short career. That same night he fell just shy of another triple-double, with 8 assists and 9 rebounds.

He was just as commanding in the second-to-last game of January. The Portland Trail Blazers had the lead throughout much of the match, in part because they had held LeBron to just 20 points in the first three quarters. Then came the fourth quarter.

Three minutes in, the score was 74–64 in favor of Portland. LeBron went up for a shot and was fouled. The bucket missed but he made both free throws to tighten it to 74–66. But Portland answered with two of their own to pull ahead 76–66.

LeBron wasn't about to let the Trail Blazers keep that lead. First, he poked a tip shot. Then he tossed in a jump shot. Then he had back-to-back-to-back three-pointers! Cleveland's score inched up, closer and closer until, with just four seconds left on the clock, they were just one point behind.

Four seconds isn't a lot of time for some players. For LeBron James, it was all the time he needed. He got his hands on the ball and with less than a second showing, rolled in a sweet reverse layup to give Cleveland the win!

"The game is not over until there are zeroes on the clock," James reminded reporters afterward.

Anyone who had seen James' fourth quarter performance that night must have been surprised to see the star player sitting on the bench the next game. Had he somehow injured himself after his 17-point tear? In fact, he had injured himself *before* it, spraining his right ankle during the second quarter of the Portland game. And yet, amazingly, he had overcome the pain to score more points single-handedly than all of the Trail Blazers combined!

No one minded when LeBron took over a game so long as it resulted in a win. But when he sat on the bench or had an unusual off-night, it became clear that the Cavaliers needed to deepen their roster and give him more help. It was with this in mind that Cleveland made a complicated mid-February trade. From the Chicago Bulls they acquired veteran forward-centers Ben Wallace and Joe Smith plus a future draft pick. From the Seattle SuperSonics they got forward-guard Wally Szczberiak and guard Delonte West. All four made an immediate, positive impact, with three of them scoring ten or more points in their first game in Cavalier uniforms.

Still, it can be difficult for a team to adjust to new players. As February turned into March, the Cavs went through a rough patch. Even on nights when LeBron scored thirty or more points, they found themselves on the losing side.

Fortunately for Cleveland fans, the Cavs still won more than they lost. By the end of the regular season, they had secured fourth place in the Eastern Conference rankings with a final record of 45–37.

The Cavaliers played their last regular season game on April 16. Knowing that they would be heading into a tough round of playoffs, they chose to rest LeBron James and other key players that match. But LeBron was the name on everybody's lips that night all the same, for it was then that he was awarded his first NBA scoring title with an average of 30.0 points per game.

In addition to his scoring power, LeBron regularly topped the lists in most aspects of the game. In 75 outings, he averaged 7.9 rebounds, 7.2 assists, 1.8 steals, and 40.4 minutes. He was the Cavs' clear leader, their go-to man in the clutch, the driving force that had spurred them to several important victories throughout the season.

But would his talent be enough to push them ahead of the competition in the post season?

The first round of the NBA playoffs began a few days after the regular season ended. The fourth-place Cavs were scheduled to play the fifth-place Washington

Wizards, a team they had beaten twice and lost to twice in the previous months. In the last of those matches, Wizard DeShawn Stevenson had made the mistake of publicly calling LeBron James "overrated."

Stevenson would soon eat his word, for in their first postseason meeting, LeBron was simply masterful.

The Wizards played him hard, bumping him, pushing him, and trash-talking him at every turn. Such aggressive play might have tripped up another, less talented player. Not LeBron. He absorbed each shove and insult and turned them into a steely determination to win. And that's just what the Cavs did, 93–86. How different might that score have looked if LeBron had caved under the pressure instead of using it? He scored 32 points in all — 20 in the second half alone, and most of those on layups!

The Cavaliers won the next game, 116–86, the widest margin for the team ever in a playoff game. But in the midst of that decisive win came an incident that nearly cost them their most valuable player.

Midway through the second quarter, LeBron got the ball near the basket. He drove the lane, intending to go for a lay-up. Suddenly, *wham!* Wizard center Brendan Haywood gave him a two-handed shove that sent James flying out of bounds!

Whistles blew and all action stopped. Was LeBron injured?

He wasn't, although he was shaken. "It was scary," he confessed later. "I knew it was going to be a tough fall. I bounced up, though."

Haywood was ejected from the game. In the referees' opinions, the Wizard hadn't fouled James to stop him from scoring. He had fouled him to stop him — period.

If that had been Haywood's intent, it backfired. James went on to score 15 more points before coming out with six minutes left in the game. In all, he chalked up 30 points and had 12 assists for a double-double, plus 9 rebounds.

Cleveland was now ahead in the series, 2–0. While a two-game lead is nice, it isn't insurmountable, as the Wizards proved in Game 3. That night, Washington embarrassed Cleveland by beating them 108–72!

The next two games were much closer and resulted in a win for each team. The series was now at 3–2 in favor of the Cavaliers. Cleveland needed just one more win to advance to the next round. If the Wizards were to stay alive, they needed to emerge victorious in the next two outings.

They didn't. Game 6 belonged to LeBron James and the Cavaliers. James posted a triple-double, with 27 points, 13 rebounds, and 13 assists. He also had 2 steals in the 105–88 series winning victory.

The Cavs–Wizards playoff was by all accounts one of the roughest in NBA postseason history. The next round would prove to be one of the toughest in Cleveland history, for their next opponents were the Boston Celtics.

After years of subpar basketball, the Celtics had surprised everyone by winning their way to a 66–16 record, the best in the league. If the Cavaliers were to beat them, they would need spectacular play from all members of the squad, particularly LeBron.

But the first meeting, the Celtics did what no other team had done that year. They shut down Cleveland's number one player. LeBron James went 2-for-18 from the floor; he scored a mere two points in the second half and missed a crucial layup in the final seconds that could have sent the game into overtime. Instead, Boston took the game, 76–72.

Maybe the pressure got to him, or maybe he was just plain exhausted from the physical play of the previous round. James himself couldn't seem to figure out what had gone wrong for him. "I missed a lot of shots I know I can make," he said after the game. "I missed layups. Those layups I've made my whole life."

Unfortunately for Cleveland fans, James's shooting didn't improve much in Game 2. He took 24 shots from the floor; he made only 6 of them for point total of 21 that night.

He had 21 points the next night, too — but this time,

those points contributed to a vastly different outcome for the Cavaliers.

Game 3 was played in Cleveland before a sellout crowd. Boosted by the cheers of their adoring and hopeful fans, the Cavaliers started out strong. Five minutes into the first quarter, they had a six point lead over the Celtics.

Then, in the sixth minute, Boston superstar Kevin Garnett ripped down a defensive rebound. He fed the ball to top scorer Paul Pierce. Pierce headed to the basket for the shot.

He didn't make it because *zip!* LeBron stole the ball!

James immediately passed to teammate Delonte West, who just as quickly returned the ball to him. James flew down the court and then — *wham!* — delivered a thunderous dunk that shook the stadium to the rafters.

That dunk set the Cavaliers on fire. By the end of the first quarter, they had jumped to a commanding 32–13 lead.

The Celtics never recovered. Cleveland took the game, 108–84. They won the next game, too, 88–77, to tie the series at two apiece. That game saw LeBron making yet another amazing play.

It came late in the fourth quarter. The Cavs had the lead, 85–72. LeBron got the ball at the top of the key and put it to the floor with a slow, methodical dribble, patiently waiting for a play to unfold.

It started seconds later when teammate Joe Smith threw a perfect screen near the free throw line. LeBron burst into action. He dribbled past Paul Pierce. He faked his way around James Posey. Then, with long strides, he skied over Kevin Garnett and jammed the ball through the hoop! He punctuated the bucket with a glare of pure determination, a look one reporter dubbed "The Baddest Man on the Planet" scowl.

"The stuff he does, it shouldn't amaze you because he is who he is, but sometimes I do get giddy inside," Cavs coach Mike Brown confessed after that play.

After two straight wins, Cleveland had all the momentum on their side. They needed only two more to put the Celtics out to pasture and reach the NBA finals for the second years in a row.

Game 4 was played in Boston and at first, it seemed Cleveland would do what few teams that year had done — namely, prevent the Celtics from winning on their home court. LeBron was a big reason why, for he had 23 points in the first half alone, two more than he had scored in any of the previous three games. If he could just keep hitting, the Cavaliers looked sure to win.

He didn't. After an impressive first two quarters, his

hot hand turned cold. He added just 11 more points to end the night with a total of 35. The Cavs ended with 89. The Celtics ended with 96 — and the win.

Two nights later, Boston looked to end their road game woes — and the series — by finally winning an away game. It didn't happen, and LeBron James was the main reason why. While it took him nearly eleven minutes to hit his first bucket, once he made it he didn't look back. Layups, free throws, jumpers, three-pointers: he was hitting everything from everywhere! He was crashing the boards, too, pulling down offensive and defensive rebounds and turning them into plays and assists. In all, he posted 32 points, 12 rebounds, and 6 assists in the 74–69 victory.

"It was either win or go home," James said later. "I'm not ready to go home."

He didn't appear ready to pack it in the next night, either. The Cavaliers were back in Boston for the deciding game of the series. Early on, the match turned into a scoring duel between offensive superstars LeBron James and Paul Pierce. Both were incredibly hot from the floor; first one would drain a jump shot from outside, then the other would drive the lane for a finger-roll layup.

Yet it seemed that James's efforts were going to fall short. The Cavaliers were behind throughout the first three quarters, sometimes by as much as ten points. It wasn't until the final minutes of the last quarter that they drew close enough to frighten the Celtics. Not surprisingly, the player who caused their panic was LeBron James.

The score was Boston 89, Cleveland 86, with two minutes, twenty seconds remaining. Pierce got the ball at mid-court and started for the hoop. James was right with him, guarding him closely, watching for his chance to make a move.

He got it! With a flash of his hand, he snared the ball from Pierce. Pierce tripped and hit the floor. LeBron, meanwhile, flew down court, trailed by Celtic players hoping to stop him before he reached the hoop. But it would have been like trying to stop a runaway train.

Wham! James took off through the air and slammed down a monstrous dunk! It was a one-point game and there were still two minutes left to play. If the Cavs could ride that momentum, they had a good chance of finally overpowering the Celtics.

They tried their best. But suddenly, LeBron's shooting went icy cold. First, he missed a three-pointer that could have put the Cavs ahead by two. The Celtics ripped down the defensive rebound and turned it into two points to give them a lead of three.

Neither team scored again for a full minute. Then, as

the clock ticked down the final minute, LeBron got the ball five feet from the hoop. He had been hitting shots like that all night. This time, however, he missed.

Seconds later, Ray Allen of the Celtics was fouled while shooting. He made both free throws to give Boston a five-point advantage.

The duel between Pierce and James turned into a battle a moment later, with Pierce fouling James during a shot. LeBron strode to the line, got the ball from the official — and, unbelievably, missed the first free throw! He made the second, however, to inch the Cavs to within four points. But with sixteen seconds remaining, Boston added two to their side when Eddie House sank two free throws.

Cleveland needed a miracle if they were going to pull off a victory. They almost got it, thanks to a three-pointer from Sasha Pavlovic off an assist from LeBron James that cut the Celtics' six-point lead to three. That lead stretched wide open again when Paul Pierce hit two free throws.

There was only one thing the Cavaliers could do now: get the ball to LeBron James. With five seconds remaining, that's exactly what they did. Twenty-six feet from the hoop, he turned and shot. The ball soared in an arc toward the basket. The crowd held its breath. Would it hit for three or miss its mark?

It missed. Cavalier Joe Smith ripped down the offensive rebound and tried to pass it back out for another shot. The ball never reached its intended receiver, however, for Eddie House raced in and stole it.

That steal sealed the game for Boston. With a final score of 97–92, the Celtics were headed to the next round of the playoffs. The Cavaliers, meanwhile, were headed home.

LeBron James had given the game everything he had. He had shot 14-for-29, made three 3-pointers, and 14 free throws for 45 points. He had pulled down 5 rebounds. He had contributed 6 assists and 2 steals.

But one player, no matter how good, does not make a winning team. In the end, Boston had pulled together and played better as a team than Cleveland, and that had made all the difference.

No one recognized that more than LeBron. "I think what we have is very good. . . . I am not disappointed in any of my teammates or any of my coaching staff," he told reporters after the loss. But he also added his belief that if the Cavs were to get better, they needed to consider making some changes to the roster.

Those changes came during the 2008 off-season. The most important was the acquisition of point guard Mo Williams, traded to the Cavaliers in exchange for shooting guard Damon Jones. Williams had been in the NBA for as long as James. He was a top playmaker who could also shoot well; in his last season with the Bucks, he averaged 17.2 points and 6.3 assists per game.

"I think Mo is a very good point guard," James said of the trade. "He can create for himself and create for others, so it's a great move. I think it's an 'A.'"

He hoped the Cavs themselves would be an "A" in the coming season, too. But first, he had to take on the best basketball teams in the world.

CHAPTER SIXTEEN

2008–2009

Olympic Dream to First-Place Team

"It's going to be like waking up on Christmas Day. All you dreamed about this whole month was having that bike you wanted, and you get down to your living room—it's there."

That's how LeBron James described his anticipation of the 2008 Summer Olympics in Beijing and his hope that Team USA would do what they'd failed to do in 2004, namely capture the gold medal. Back then, he'd watched from the bench as his teammates floundered and came home with just the bronze. Now, "it's the gold, or it's failure," he said.

And failing was not something LeBron planned to do. So in mid-August, he added his skill, power, and determination to win to a talented roster that included Kobe Bryant, Dwight Howard, Carmelo Anthony, Dwyane Wade, and Carlos Boozer.

Team USA—or the Redeem Team, as some in the press called it—paved a clear path through the early rounds by defeating China, Angola, Greece, Spain, Germany, and Australia. Most of the scores were lop-sided, as U.S. players chalked up 30 or more points than their opponents. The same held true in the semifinals, where the U.S. beat Argentina 101–81 to reach the gold-medal round.

There, they faced Spain, whom they had defeated earlier by a score of 119–82. If they had expected a similar romp this match, they quickly learned that Spain had other ideas. In the fourth quarter, the Spanish players were breathing down the U.S. team's neck, just two points shy of a tie.

That was as close as they came, however. Kobe Bryant and Dwyane Wade stepped up their already high-powered offensive drive to sink 13 points combined, including Wade's fourth three-pointer of the game. Final score: U.S. 118, Spain 107.

While Wade was the hero of the gold-medal victory, with 27 points and enough three-pointers to give the U.S. an Olympic record for the most threes ever scored (13) in a finals series, LeBron had contributed firepower as well, with 14 points and 6 rebounds. "Much respect to Spain, but U.S. is back on top again," LeBron said with satisfaction.

After the Olympics, the players returned to their NBA teams to begin preparations for the 2008–2009 season. James was looking forward to a great year. Yet, after the preseason, the Cavs won only three of the eight games played.

Fans needn't have worried. While Cleveland dropped its first regular-season match to the champion Boston Celtics, they won twenty of the next twenty-two for a mid-December record of twenty wins and just three losses! In that time, James racked up three 40-point games, four 30-point games, and eleven 20-point games. But unlike in years past, when he was often the sole offensive threat, this season he had plenty of backup in Mo Williams, Anderson Varejao, Zydrunas Ilgauskas, and Delonte West, all of whom were regularly scoring in the double digits.

Their record strengthened even more in the weeks leading up to the All-Star break. On February 4, the Cavaliers won their thirty-ninth game, at Madison Square Garden against the New York Knicks.

And what a game it was for LeBron James! He had 10 rebounds and 11 assists. He also had 52 points, earning his twenty-first career triple-double. His point total was the second-highest for a triple-double in NBA history; only the great Wilt Chamberlain had more, with 53, and that had been more than forty years earlier!

James was the high-scorer for his team in the NBA All-Star Game later that month, hitting 20. Unfortunately, the East had no answer for the West's one-two Kobe Bryant–Shaquille O'Neal punch. They lost 146–119.

LeBron's shooting hand had been hot for most of the season, but on February 20, it was absolutely smoking. The Cavs faced the Bucks that night in Milwaukee. The Bucks were surprisingly strong against Cleveland, and at halftime they had the lead, 57–51. After the break, however, James stepped in.

Swish! A 15-foot bank shot. *Swish!* A three-pointer from 27 feet out. *Swish! Swish! Swish!* Three 26-foot three-pointers in a row, and then *swish* again for a bucket good for 2 more points! In less than three minutes, LeBron James had scored 16 points to put Cleveland ahead, 67–61!

And he wasn't done yet—far from it. Free throws, layups, jump shots, more threes — James ended the evening with 55 points, including eight three-pointers, the most threes he'd made in his career in a single game. He added 5 rebounds and 9 assists as well to spur his team to a 111–103 win, their forty-second of the season.

"It was almost like watching a video game," teammate Ilgauskas said of James's performance.

"Just got in the zone, man," was LeBron's explanation for his unbelievable shooting.

In March, James didn't just get in the zone — he stayed in it night after night after night. On the seventh, he chalked up his fourth triple-double of the season.

On the tenth, he had another, and on the twelfth, he made it three in a row! Even better, each effort ended with a hash mark in Cleveland's win column.

"I hope everybody and anybody out there is talking about him," Cavs coach Mike Brown said of his superstar, "and talking about him for MVP because he deserves it."

Proof that he deserved it came with every outing. He added yet another triple-double to bring his season total to seven, and he had two other games of 40-plus points.

Fueled by his talent, the Cavs finished the season at the top of the league with 66 wins and 16 losses, their best franchise record ever. James's year-end averages were among his best, too: 28.4 points, 7.6 rebounds, and 7.2 assists per game in 81 games. As Coach Brown had hoped — and as many had predicted — when the MVP votes were tallied, LeBron James had the highest number: 1,172.

"If I said I didn't enjoy this award I'd be lying," the twenty-four-year-old basketball superstar said. "Hard work pays off and dreams do come true."

LeBron had one more dream he promised to make come true for himself, his teammates, and all Cleveland fans.

"We're going to bring y'all that championship."

But was it a promise he and the Cavs could keep?

★ CHAPTER SEVENTEEN ★

2009

Great Expectations

Four straight. That's how the Cavaliers defeated their first-round opponents, the Detroit Pistons. It's how they took care of the Atlanta Hawks in the Conference Semifinals, too. LeBron James was positively masterful in all eight games. No-look passes, dunks from all angles, layups, fadeaways, three-pointers, assists through triple-team defense — the newly minted MVP had all the moves at all the right times. His shooting was strong from start to finish, with tallies ranging from a low of 25 points to a high of 47.

But the fight wasn't over yet. Up next was one of the Cavs' toughest rivals, the Orlando Magic and their amazing center, Dwight Howard. Howard had been particularly effective at shutting down LeBron James's offense in their past meetings. If he brought that same kind of power to this round in the playoffs, then the Cavaliers were going to have to work much harder to advance to the Finals.

Game 1 was played in Cleveland before a crowd of more than twenty thousand fans. The Cavs jumped to an early lead in the first quarter, outscoring the Magic 33 to 19. Orlando matched them nearly point-for-point in the second, but Cleveland emerged with a 15-point advantage at the halftime break.

The teams raced neck and neck into the final seconds. With just fourteen seconds on the clock, Rashard Lewis stuck a three-pointer to give Orlando a one-point lead, 107–106.

Cleveland immediately called a time-out. They knew they had just enough time to make a final play. They returned to the court and inbounded the ball. LeBron got it just past half court. He circled around the key to the right and drove to the hoop. A layup? No! James jumped up, but he passed the ball back out to Williams, who fired it to Delonte West behind the three-point arc. West shot — and missed!

There was a scramble under the basket. The refs called a jump ball between James and Orlando's Hedo Turkoglu with one second remaining. Williams got the tip and shot from the top of the key. The ball soared toward the basket, hit the rim — and rebounded off! The Magic won, 107–106!

How did LeBron James feel about the outcome? "Unacceptable."

Game 2 started out much the same way Game 1

had, with the Cavaliers earning a big lead in the first quarter and the Magic surging from behind to narrow the margin by the end of the third. Going into the fourth quarter, the score was Cleveland 75, Orlando 69. Six minutes into the fourth quarter, it was all tied up at 84. The Cavs managed to stay one small step ahead for most of the remaining minutes.

Then, with just thirty seconds left, Turkoglu hit a three that knotted the score, 93–93. Twenty-nine seconds later, it was Turkoglu again for two. The Magic had the lead!

The Cavs needed a miracle to pull off the win. Luckily, they had one in the form of LeBron James.

With one second showing on the clock and the score 95–93, Williams took the ball to the sidelines by the Cavs' hoop. He searched for the open man to pass to — and found James cutting to the top of the key! He fired a pass. James caught it outside the three-point line and, in one smooth move, he turned and shot just as the buzzer sounded.

"LeBron, for three, for the win," the announcer called excitedly as he and everyone else in the arena followed the ball's arcing path. Then — *Yes! LeBron James! At the buzzer!*

James jumped up and down like a little boy, he was so happy. "I told Mo whatever it was going to take for me, I was going to come get the ball," he told reporters

115

afterward. "It is the biggest shot I have made in my career."

After two slow starts in the previous meetings, the Magic raced into the lead in Game 3, holding the Cavs to just 17 points in the first quarter. They needed to do more to hold LeBron James, however, for he scored 8 of those 17 points.

James added 10 more in the second quarter, which helped the Cavs draw within one of the Magic. But despite his best efforts — he would finish with 41 for the night, plus 7 rebounds, 9 assists, 2 steals, and a block — Orlando outscored Cleveland in the third to pull away again. In the fourth, they sealed the deal by knocking down 31 points to the Cavs' 26 for a final score of 99–89.

The Cavaliers were now down in the series two games to one. They came very close to making it all even in the next game, forcing the game into extra minutes, thanks in large part to James's outstanding scoring. And in the final moment of those extra minutes, with the Cavs down 116–114, it looked like he would pull another rabbit out of his hat for Cleveland when he shot a three-pointer at the buzzer.

But this time, there would be no miracle. The shot missed, and the Magic had their third victory.

Cleveland was down, but not out. Before their hometown crowd, the Cavaliers picked the Magic apart to win Game 5 112–102.

"It was win or go home," James, who posted triple-double numbers, said matter-of-factly.

Clearly, the MVP wasn't ready to pack his bags just yet. So instead, Orlando packed them for him and for the rest of the Cavs. Behind a monstrous 40-point, 14-rebound game from center Dwight Howard, the Magic routed their opponents 103–90 to advance into their first Finals since 1995.

While the Magic celebrated with their fans beneath a rain of confetti, LeBron James bowed his head and left the arena without saying a word to anyone. His quest had once again fallen short.

CHAPTER EIGHTEEN

2009–2010

"It's Over"

The Cleveland Cavaliers arguably had one of the best players in the league and an incredible season in 2008–2009. And yet, they had not reached the Finals. The problem, they thought, was that they had no real answer when powerful centers like Dwight Howard challenged LeBron James. So, after their season ended, they remedied that situation by acquiring a player used to handling big men underneath the hoop: Shaquille O'Neal.

O'Neal had been a star in the NBA for more than a decade and a half. He had a long and storied history in the postseason, including four championship victories and three Finals MVP awards. Although he had been plagued by injuries in recent years, he was still a considerable force on the court — and, by all reports, delighted to have the opportunity to play with LeBron James.

James, too, seemed happy to have O'Neal in a Cleveland uniform. "I have a lot of respect for him and his game," he told the press. "It will be a real honor to play with Shaq as my teammate, and I look forward to another great season with the Cavs."

Considering that both James and Shaq were used to being the focus of their teams' attention and plays, their partnering made some Cavalier fans uneasy. Was the court big enough for two such enormous talents? Even with Shaq's repeated statements that he was in Cleveland to be a role player, not the sole player, it wasn't until the Cavs had several wins under their belts that Cleveland relaxed.

Unfortunately, Shaq wasn't on the court with James for the whole season. After a strong start, he was sidelined for several games with a shoulder strain. He was forced to sit out the latter part of the schedule, too, after tearing a ligament in his thumb.

The Cavs would have liked to have Shaq on the court, but his absence didn't bring them down. They ended with a final record of 61-21 — not quite as good as the previous year, but still good enough for their second straight season in the league's top spot.

James had been spectacular, finishing near or above his best averages with 29.7 points, 7.3 rebounds, 8.2 assists, 1.6 steals, and 1.0 block per game. On March

19, 2010, he earned a place in the NBA records as the youngest player ever to reach 15,000 points; he finished 2010 with 2,258 for a career total of 15,251.

He sat out the last four matches in order to be well-rested for the postseason. The rest must have been good for him, for he was all but unstoppable in the first round of the playoffs against the Chicago Bulls. He was the top scorer in four out of the five games. In Game 4, he earned his fifth triple-double of his postseason career with 37 points, 12 rebounds, and 11 assists, and he hit an unbelievable half-court buzzer-beater in the third quarter.

Not that Cleveland needed the points or the inspiration at that point; the Cavs shredded the Bulls, 121–98, to go up 3–1 in the series.

The next night, however, LeBron scored just 19 points. Cleveland still landed the victory to advance to the next round, but it was a hard-fought battle — so hard-fought, in fact, that it left the Cavaliers' star player clutching his right elbow and grimacing in pain. Exactly how James had injured himself, he couldn't say. Instead, he brushed it aside to focus on the team's next challenge, the Boston Celtics.

The Conference Semifinals opened in Cleveland with a solid 101–93 win for the Cavaliers. The second game was another story. The Celtics absolutely destroyed the Cavs in the third quarter, holding them to just 12 points in 12 minutes. Of those 12 points, LeBron made just 4. The sudden drop made many speculate that the elbow injury was bothering him more than he was willing to admit.

He might have been in pain, but what troubled him more was the 104–86 loss that tied the series at a game apiece. So he made sure that the Cavaliers took the upper hand right away in Game 3 with an offensive onslaught that ended with him shooting 21 points in the first quarter alone!

That same night, Cleveland delivered Boston's worst home playoff defeat in the franchise's history, 124–95. The Cavaliers now were ahead in the series 2–1.

The Celtics weren't ready to roll over and die just yet, however. With their spunky guard Rajon Rondo weaving in and out of the Cleveland players on his way to a game-high 29 points, the Boston club churned out a 97–87 win. And in Game 5, they turned the tables on the Cavs, handing them *their* worst home-court postseason defeat in their history with a 120–88 drubbing!

LeBron tried not to let the loss — or the catcalls and boos that followed him out of the arena — get him down. There were still two games left to play in the series, after all, and every possibility that Cleveland could win them both to advance to the Finals.

Unfortunately, though, Boston finished what they'd

started, beating the Cavaliers 94–85 to win the Eastern Conference.

"The fact that it's over right now is definitely a surprise to me," James said afterward. "A friend of mine told me, 'I guess you've got to go through a lot of nightmares before you realize your dream.' That's what's going on for me individually right now."

What that friend might not have known was that, for Cleveland fans, the nightmare was just beginning. With the season's end, LeBron James became a free agent. That meant that he could sign with whatever team offered him the best opportunity for future success.

☆ CHAPTER NINETEEN ☆

Summer of 2010

The Decision

Wild speculation about where he would go — if he left Cleveland at all — clogged sports networks and blogs in the days after the Cavaliers' elimination from the playoffs. Many sports analysts reported that LeBron was headed to the New York Knicks because of the city's huge sports market and the Knicks' lack of star power. Others were sure he was headed to Dallas to team with All-Star Dirk Nowitzki, while more still thought he'd land with the New Jersey Nets, who were planning to move the team to Brooklyn, New York. James recognized that his announcement would be big news, and he treated it as such by scheduling a full hour of prime-time television in which to make it.

The day Lebron James made his decision will go down in sports history as the day he changed the landscape of basketball and perhaps all sports. *The Decision*, as the show was dubbed, aired live on ESPN on July 8, 2010. Looking uncharacteristically ill-at-ease before the camera, LeBron answered questions posed by interviewer Jim Gray before finally coming to the main point of the show.

"The answer to the question everybody wants to know," Gray said. "LeBron, what's your decision?"

James hesitated and stumbled over the beginning of his reply before finally answering. "This fall, I'm going to take my talents to South Beach and join the Miami Heat."

He went on to list his reasons for making the choice, including his desire to team up with Dwyane Wade and Chris Bosh, two stars of the NBA he felt offered him the best chance for multiple titles. "I feel like it's going to give me the best opportunity to win, and to win for multiple years," James said. "Not only just to win in the regular season, or just to win five games in a row, or three games in a row. I want to be able to win championships. I feel like I can compete down there."

Never before had three superstars chosen less money to play together with the sole purpose of winning championships and perhaps creating a dynasty, but both current and former NBA professionals as well as the media were quick to criticize the Heat, Wade, Bosh, and especially LeBron James.

Michael Jordan, perhaps the greatest player to play the game, disagreed with *The Decision*, saying, "There's no way, with hindsight, I would've ever called up Larry [Bird], called up Magic [Johnson], and said, 'Hey, look, let's get together and play on one team.'" Jordan also recognized the changes in the league that had occurred since his playing days, admitting, "But that's . . . Things are different. I can't say that's a bad thing. It's an opportunity these kids have today. In all honesty, I was trying to beat those guys."

Charles Barkley, the outspoken TV analyst for *Inside the NBA* and former All-Star power forward for the 76ers and the Suns, wasn't as understanding. "He'll never be Jordan," Barkley maintained on a Miami-area radio show. "This clearly takes him out of the conversation. He can win as much as he wants to," he added. "There would have been something honorable about staying in Cleveland and trying to win it as 'The Man.' . . . LeBron, if he would've in Cleveland, and if he could've got a championship there, it would have been over the top for his legacy, just one in Cleveland. No matter how many he wins in Miami, it clearly is Dwyane Wade's team."

But for heartbroken Cleveland fans, no explanation would ever be good enough. King James was leaving them, and taking *their* best chances for a title with him. From the time LeBron James entered the league, he has always been one of the most talked-about sports celebrities in the world. Before *The Decision*, most of that talk was complimentary, full of praise for his mind-blowing achievements on the court. But afterward, a lot of that talk turned to trash as those who once worshipped him as a hero now treated him like a pariah.

And sometimes that's just part of being a public figure, but regardless of how he handled the announcement or what effect his choice had on the Cavaliers and the city of Cleveland, James was still one of the best basketball players to grace the court in many years. His talent elevated the game to a new level, inspired other players to reach higher for their goals, and brought joy to those who watched him play the game he loves.

James brings joy to people off the court as well. Soon after turning pro in 2003, he started his own charitable organization, the LeBron James Family Foundation, aimed at giving single-parent families like the one he grew up in the support they need to raise successful children. He donated $200,000 to help victims of Hurricanes Katrina and Rita in 2005. In 2009, he pledged $1 million to ONEXONE, a foundation that addresses the need for children throughout the world to have clean water, food, health care, education, and play in order to live happy, healthy lives.

He has given back to kids in his local communities time and again. He contributed thousands of backpacks filled with school supplies to Ohio schools, and he donated sporting equipment to community centers so that underprivileged kids can have better education and better access to sports. A big kid himself sometimes, he helped towns buy and build playgrounds so children will have places where they can play safely. He's been a major player in the King for Kids Bike-a-thon, an event he helped develop and in which he's taken part nearly every year since 2004.

Why does he do all of this? His answer is simple and from the heart: "It's great to see the smiles on kids' faces."

And to those Ohio fans who turned their backs on him after *The Decision*, he had a special message, one that he hoped would help them forgive. It wasn't an apology, but rather an expression of his feelings for his hometown and a reassurance that, no matter where he played, he would never forget his roots:

"For all of my life, I have lived in Akron — and for that, I am truly a lucky man. It was here where I first learned how to play basketball, and where I met the people who would become my lifelong friends and mentors. . . . It's where I started, and it's where I will always come back to. . . . You mean everything to me."

Such a heartfelt statement might give Ohio fans hope that someday not too far in the future, LeBron James would return to wear the Cavalier uniform again.

★ CHAPTER TWENTY ★

2010–2011

A Whole New Ballgame

LeBron James started his tenure with the Heat by announcing it to 9.95 million viewers during the poorly received television event, and then he traveled to his new home in Florida for his introduction to Heat fans. This was the first time LeBron had ever lived outside Ohio in his life. The backlash from *The Decision* and the excessive celebration that followed only intensified the spotlight on the small forward.

To make matters worse, the Heat got off to a slow start to begin the 2010–2011 season, losing eight of their first eighteen games and twice to the Eastern Conference rival Celtics, though James dropped 31 and 35 points, respectively, in each game. Because of the lack of team chemistry, the media began to question James's leadership on and off the court. Dwyane Wade had won a championship in Miami already, and it had been his team for the previous seven seasons. James was the newcomer here, but still everyone expected him to be the leader of the team. Those with insider knowledge of the Heat knew that it would take the team time to learn how to play together. Even James acknowledged this after their first loss to the Celtics. "It's a feel-out process," James said. "When you have so many options, it's something I'm not accustomed to, having that many threats out on the court at the same time."

By December, the pieces began to fall into place, and the Heat won fifteen of sixteen games that month. One of the Heat's biggest games came early in the month, when the Heat traveled to Cleveland to take on the Cavaliers in LeBron's first game home since he left. As expected, James was showered with a chorus of boos throughout the game, which would later be known as "The Return." In fact, the fans booed every time James touched the ball. The fans wanted to make sure LeBron James knew exactly how they felt after he'd left them for another team, but James had a statement to make of his own.

Great players respond to intense pressure with greatness, and James responded to the fans in a big way. He went off that night, scoring 24 of his 38 points in the third quarter, adding 5 rebounds and 8 assists in a 118–90 thumping of the Cavaliers. From the first tip-off to the final buzzer, LeBron showed off his massive skills on both sides of the ball. When the game was over, James showed what a tremendous professional he has always been. During a postgame interview when TNT analyst Craig Sager asked what he would like to say to the fans, James responded, "Seven great years! Loved every part, loved every moment. . . . As a team we tried our best to bring a championship to this city and . . . play hard every night. I have the utmost respect for this franchise, utmost respect for these fans."

As the season progressed, so, too, did the chemistry of the Heat. The team played better and finished stronger every game. By the All-Star break, the Heat were on fire. Both LeBron and Dwyane Wade were selected to start for the Eastern Conference, and Chris Bosh was selected as a reserve. Not since Shaquille O'Neal and Wade were All-Stars had two Heat players started for the Eastern Conference, and it was the first time that three players were named All-Stars in franchise history.

CHAPTER TWENTY-ONE

2010–2011

2011 NBA Playoffs

The Heat finished the season red-hot and steamrolled their way into the playoffs, winning 15 of their last 18 games with LeBron averaging 28.7 points per game over that period.

The Heat's 58–24 record in the season was the third-best in the Heat's history, good enough for a second seed in the East and a first-round matchup with the Philadelphia 76ers. The underdog Sixers weren't much of a challenge. The Heat would lose the fourth game of the series but ultimately cruise to a 4–1 series win.

Dwyane Wade had made it his mission to knock the Celtics out of the playoffs, and LeBron was more than happy to help him. The two All-Stars teamed up to carry the offensive load for the Heat. The Heat won the series 4–1 and headed straight into a matchup with the Chicago Bulls and their star point guard, Derrick Rose.

The Bulls swept the Heat during the regular season and dominated Game 1 of the Eastern Conference

131

Finals, beating the Heat 103–82. Rose dropped 28 points, hitting from behind the line and owning the lane despite having committed three turnovers in the early stages of the game.

Luckily for the Heat, Rose got in early foul trouble in Game 2 and never got into a solid rhythm like he had in Game 1, and that left the door open for LeBron James to take over late in the fourth quarter. The Heat won 85–75. After scoring only 15 points in the first game, LeBron averaged 28.5 points per game over the next four games, which the Heat won, ultimately taking the series 4–1 with their defensive play. They were the Eastern Conference Champions, and they would now face the Dallas Mavericks in the NBA Finals.

It's a great accomplishment just to make it to the finals, but LeBron wouldn't settle for anything less than a championship, saying, "We've still got work to do. We'll look at this moment tonight, have a little bit of time tomorrow to go over this moment, what we just accomplished. But we get ready for Dallas very soon."

Led by Dirk Nowitzki, Dallas's All-Star power forward, the Mavericks were a strong defensive team with a deep bench. Their center, Tyson Chandler, manned the lane while former Sixth Man of the Year Jason Terry provided long-range firepower. This was as deep a team as the Heat had seen in the playoffs yet.

LeBron started the series with a team-high 24 points

to go with 9 rebounds and 5 assists in the first game. But it was the little things that made James's first NBA Finals win so special. LeBron dove for every loose ball, hitting the deck hard on more than one occasion, and challenged every shot in his area. He set the tone for what would be a physical series early in Game 1 when he fouled Terry hard on a dunk attempt, sending the guard crashing to the pine.

Game 2 seemed to be headed the same way, with LeBron continuing his strong play, running circles around the slower Dallas team and forcing the Mavs into 18 turnovers. Up by 15 points late in the fourth quarter, Wade and LeBron took their feet off the gas, letting Nowitzki and Terry mount a comeback. The Mavericks scored the next 18 points and took the lead on a Nowitzki three with 26.7 seconds remaining. Backup point guard Mario Chalmers hit a three with 24 seconds left in the game to tie it up at 93–93. But the veteran Jason Kidd worked the clock, getting Nowitzki the ball with just under ten seconds to go. Nowitzki hit an easy layup off a nasty spin move as the clock wound down to even the series at 1–1.

Game 3 was not a great game offensively for LeBron. He managed a mere 17 points on 6-for-14 shooting, including hitting just one of four from behind the arc and adding only 3 rebounds, though he did have 9 assists. The Heat ultimately won the game, 88–86, behind some stingy defense and a bit of timely offense from Wade and Bosh.

With a one-game series lead, the wheels fell off completely for the Heat in Game 4. James had his worst game of the series, scoring only 8 points. "I've got to do a better job of being more assertive offensively," James said. "I'm confident in my ability. It's just about going out there and knocking them down." Wade's 32 points and Bosh's 24 points were the only reason the game was as close as it was, because the rest of the team underperformed considerably.

The Game 4 loss not only evened the series at 2–2, but it also marked a major momentum shift for the Mavericks. The Heat would not win another game and would end up losing the Finals in six games. For the series, LeBron averaged 10 points less per game than his season average, and many of his staunchest critics were vindicated by his poor Finals performances, arguing that LeBron was afraid to take the big shot and didn't have the support of his team. While the Heat lost the Finals as a team, all the criticism landed squarely on LeBron's shoulders, as it had the whole season. *The Decision* continued to haunt James.

The King would have the off-season to think about what he needed to do to win that elusive NBA Championship. With the threat of a league-wide lockout and the starting date of the 2011–2012 season uncertain, James would have to wait even longer to get another chance at the title.

★ CHAPTER TWENTY-TWO ★

2011–2012

The Lockout Season and Going for the Win

The 2011–2012 season almost didn't happen. Disputes over a hard salary cap, revenue sharing between owners and players, and a lack of productive negotiations on a new Collective Bargaining Agreement (CBA) led to the owners locking out the players on July 1, 2011. For 160 days, the two sides could not come to an agreement, and the lockout ultimately cost the league a total of 240 games (16 per team) and the first two months of the season.

A new schedule was created that cut the season from 82 to 66 games, with the first game scheduled on Christmas Day between the Mavericks and the Heat, a rematch of the previous year's Finals. On the first day of free agency, the Heat re-signed Juwan Howard and James Jones, as well as restricted free-agent point guard Mario Chalmers. The Heat also added two veterans to help the team off the bench, signing Shane Battier, a defensive-minded small forward, on the same day that former fourth-overall draft pick Eddy Curry signed.

The Heat went 19–6 over the first 25 games, the Heat's best start in franchise history, and headed into the All-Star break with a 27–7 record. This team had broken another franchise record, due in large part to the King's strong play as he was averaging 27.1 points, 7.9 rebounds, and 6.2 assists per game. For the second straight year, LeBron and D-Wade were named to the All-Star Game as starters, while Bosh was named an All-Star reserve for the Eastern Conference.

The Heat entered the postseason of 2011 as the second seed in the East behind the Bulls and drew the New York Knicks as their first-round matchup. The heavily favored Heat easily dispatched the Knicks and won the series 4–1. The next series against the Indiana Pacers was much more difficult, and it almost ended LeBron's season early.

The Indiana Pacers had a breakout performance the previous season and they followed it up with an even stronger 2011–2012 season, entering the playoffs as the third seed just behind Miami. The Pacers had cruised past Orlando, winning the series 4–1, to face the determined Heat in the Conference Semifinals.

The series with Indiana started off with a scare for the Heat. During the latter stages of the first half of Game 1 Chris Bosh went up for a dunk and quickly fell to the court in pain. The Heat went into halftime unsure what was wrong with their best interior player. It turned out that Bosh had a severe abdominal strain and would be out the rest of the series, and maybe the rest of the postseason. James and Wade put the Heat on their shoulders, combining for 42 points in the second half to win the game 95–86.

In Games 2 and 3, the Heat sorely missed their All-Star power forward, but late misses and poor shooting were the real reason for their back-to-back defeats. James scored 28 points and grabbed 9 rebounds in the second game, but missed two free throws in the last minutes of a three-point loss that had some believing the Pacers were going to win the series. Game 3 was a total blowout, and everyone was criticizing James, despite the fact that Wade shot 15 percent from the field and scored only 5 points.

In Indianapolis for Game 4, the Heat needed a big game from their stars. LeBron James decided to make history. He was all over the court. James scored 40 points, with 18 rebounds and 9 assists. Only Elgin Baylor had ever had that good of a game in the playoffs. Wade and James by themselves scored a combined 43 points in the second half, 4 more than the entire Pacers team, and the duo outrebounded Indiana 19–18.

This extraordinary performance by LeBron changed the entire series and landed him in the record books.

The Heat would come from behind to win the last three games and move on to the Eastern Conference Finals.

The biggest question for the Heat going into their series with the Boston Celtics was: When would Chris Bosh be healthy enough to play? Despite Bosh's absence, the Heat had actually continued their strong defense and had gotten some offensive help from Haslem and Ronny Turiaf. But the Celtics front-court included Kevin Garnett, and the Heat desperately needed Bosh back.

The Heat won the first two games at home to go up two games against Boston. The best part was that King James continued his outstanding play. Kevin Garnett, Rajon Rondo, Paul Pierce, and Ray Allen had already won an NBA Championship together in 2008, and returning to Boston awakened something in the Celtics' four best players that tipped the series in their favor. The Celtics won the next game—and the next, and the next. The Heat went completely cold on offense. They missed shot after shot for long stretches. Not even LeBron could score enough. If the Heat tried to stop Rondo, then Garnett would go off. If it wasn't Garnett, then it was Pierce or Allen. Without Bosh, Garnett was too much for Haslem. There were just too many mismatches on the court. The Celtics quickly realized that they couldn't keep James from scoring, so they focused on shutting down Dwyane Wade and the other members of the Heat. And it seemed to work. LeBron put up big points, averaging 31 points per game over the three losses, but James and the Heat couldn't find a way to win, even when Bosh returned in Game 5.

In a do-or-die Game 6, LeBron took over. He dominated the first half, hitting spinning fadeaways with hands in his face, driving to the rim with ease, and slamming home a missed shot by Bosh that shook the rim. James had 30 points in the first half and shot 19 of 26 for 45 points in 45 minutes of play. It was his eleventh 40-point playoff game, and it pulled the Heat back from the brink of elimination. James knew the pressure was on him, and he responded big.

"The shots he was making was unbelievable. He really put on an MVP performance tonight," said D-Wade of LeBron's Game 6 performance.

James set the standard again in the third Game 7 of his career. The game was back and forth until midway through the fourth quarter, when Miami's Big Three took charge and outscored Boston 28–15. LeBron ended the game with 31 points. He also silenced his critics who said he couldn't win when it counted most. In fact, he did it two games in a row, and sent his team to a second consecutive NBA Finals.

Nothing about winning a championship is ever easy. You can have the best player in the NBA on your team and still not win. But great players seem to find a way to overcome any obstacle.

The Oklahoma Thunder were having a great season, and that was partly because of how they had spent their extended off-season during the lockout. A core group of players including Kevin Durant, James Harden, Serge Ibaka, and Thabo Sefolosha had all played exhibition games across the country to stay fresh. Kevin Durant, the reigning three-time NBA scoring champ, was the biggest threat to the Heat's championship hopes, but Miami also had to game-plan for Russell Westbrook, the other All-Star on the team. The Thunder rolled through the playoffs by sweeping the Dallas Mavericks, the previous year's NBA champs, then taking out the Lakers and beating the first-seed San Antonio Spurs. The Thunder were scorching hot by the time the Finals started.

The Heat had come from behind to win two playoff series. They trailed 2–1 to Indiana, and everyone thought their season was over. Then they were down 3–2 to the Celtics. So when they dropped Game 1 to the Thunder, they were in a familiar position.

Game 2 in Oklahoma City started smoothly for the Heat, who built a 12-point lead during the first quarter and led until midway through the third quarter, when Durant began to catch fire, draining threes and taking it to the rack for a total of 32 points that night.

Once again, it was up to LeBron. The King stepped

up in the fourth quarter. He was fouled with time winding down. He hit two clutch free throws with seven seconds on the clock to give the Heat a 100–96 win and even the series at 1–1. It was LeBron's best overall finals performance of his career.

It was back to Miami for Game 3, where LeBron posted 29 points and 14 rebounds to go with D-Wade's 25 points, 7 rebounds, and 7 assists. The Heat won the game 91–85 behind the strong play of their two stars and were only two games from the championship.

During Game 4, LeBron pushed through painful leg cramps to lead the Heat with 26 points and 12 assists. His defending helped keep Durant in check all night. The Heat won the game 104–98 to take a 3–1 series lead.

By Game 5, it seemed like LeBron's first NBA Championship was destined. At halftime, Miami was up by 10 points. By the end of the third quarter, LeBron and company had built a 95–71 lead, and the Heat could smell the Finals trophy. LeBron put up a triple-double that night, hitting 9 of 19 for 26 points, grabbing 11 boards, and adding 11 dimes. The Heat ultimately won the game 121–106. LeBron James finally had his championship, and he added another first when he was unanimously voted the NBA Finals MVP.

"You know, my dream has become a reality now, and it's the best feeling I ever had," James said.

★ CHAPTER TWENTY-THREE ★

2012–2013

Back-to-Back

LeBron James, Dwyane Wade, and Chris Bosh had all promised championships when they chose to sign with the Miami Heat. Not one, but many. Everyone knew that another title was the goal. Before the parties had ended, before the fans had finished celebrating, before LeBron had time to let it all sink in, he was back to work. Fresh off another gold medal win at the 2012 Summer Olympics in London (Wade and Bosch didn't compete due to injuries), LeBron returned to Miami, ready to chase another Finals trophy. When the season began, everyone expected to see the Heat win.

But the season didn't get off to the strongest start. However, after a February 1 loss to the Pacers, something changed, something clicked, and the Heat stopped losing. They didn't lose at home or on the road for 27 games, from February 3 to March 25, 2013. The Heat only lost two more games the rest of the regular season. In the Heat's 99–94 home win over the

Charlotte Bobcats, LeBron had a historic shooting night. He only scored 31 points, which might seem paltry in an era of inflated points-per-game stats, but he did it with 13-of-14 shooting that night. He only missed one shot and one free throw all game.

Over the last 39 games of the season, the Heat's record was 37–2. Their only two losses were against the Bulls, who broke the winning streak with a 101–97 loss, and the Knicks, who played Miami tougher than any other team had that season. After the start of February, the Heat posted an incredible .948 winning percentage. The 27-game winning streak was the second longest in NBA history behind the 1971–72 LA Lakers' 33-game streak. LeBron was the top scorer in 14 of the 27 games and was the assists leader in 16 games. The Heat only lost four games at home that whole season and became the fourteenth team to finish with a winning percentage more than .800 in a season. This catapulted the Heat into the postseason with a deserved swagger.

The Heat entered the playoffs as the number one seed in the Eastern Conference. Their first matchup was against the Milwaukee Bucks, a team that had finished the regular season with a losing record. The Heat swept the Bucks in four games. The Heat then sent the Bulls on vacation with a 4–1 series win and set up a meeting with the third-seed Pacers in the Eastern Conference Finals.

The lead alternated 17 times in Game 1 against Indianapolis. There was a total of 18 ties. The Heat would take the lead only to have the Pacers surge ahead. The Heat were up 92–89 with less than 10 seconds left in the game, but then Paul George hit a three-point shot to force overtime. During overtime, the lead changed hands four more times. But no one contested LeBron on the last play of the game. The Heat won 103–102. James ended up with a 30-10-10 triple-double.

"Welcome to the Eastern Conference Finals," Coach Spoelstra said. "Back and forth the whole way."

The entire series was back and forth. The Heat won Game 1 and then each of the odd numbered games. The Pacers took a close Game 2 and then all the even numbered games. The only constant was that LeBron James was the leading scorer in each game.

It came down to a decisive Game 7. Just four quarters and the Heat would make their third straight final. LeBron dropped 12 of the Heat's 33 second-quarter points to help the Heat take a 52–37 lead at the half. LeBron finished with a game-high 32 points, adding 8 rebounds, and the Heat stomped the Pacers 99–76.

Playing the Spurs in 2013 might have been the Heat's biggest challenge that season. The Spurs' star, the quiet big man from Wake Forest University, was Tim Duncan, and he had been the heart of San Antonio for the last 15 years. He had won four NBA titles for the Spurs.

144

He was a back-to-back league MVP, a three-time Finals MVP, a fourteen-time All-Star, the All-Star MVP in 2000, and Rookie of the Year in 1998. A guaranteed first ballot Hall of Famer, Duncan had been one of the best players in the NBA for his entire career.

The Heat had the home-court advantage, which meant that San Antonio wanted to steal one of the first two games before heading to Texas for three games. The Spurs' best player that night was point guard Tony Parker, who spent the game breaking out his spin move and hitting off-balance acrobatic shots to help the Spurs win Game 1, 92–88.

The Heat responded with a blowout 103–85 win in Game 2, despite LeBron shooting only 41 percent from the field. Then San Antonio absolutely crushed the Heat 113–77 in the third game as the Spurs hit 16 threes and outscored Miami 63–33 in the second half. With the momentum clearly in favor of the Spurs, LeBron James, Dwyane Wade, and Chris Bosh collectively put together a great team performance to tie the series in Game 4. The Big Three combined to score 85 of the Heat's 109 points—78 percent of the total points that night. They were unstoppable.

"It was on our shoulders," James said. "We had to figure out how to win the game for us and play at the highest level. When all three of us are clicking, together, we're very tough . . . to beat."

Parker scored 26 points in Game 5 while Duncan added another 17 points. The 114–104 win put the Spurs 3–2. LeBron and company would have to win two straight games to win another title. But at least both games were in South Beach.

Game 6 was one of the greatest games in NBA Finals history. LeBron carried the team for most of the game and helped the Heat come back from a 10-point deficit, but he started to miss during the fourth quarter, so his teammates picked things up. Ray Allen tied the game with five seconds left with a catch-and-shoot three-pointer in the corner to force overtime. He changed the entire series with that one shot, and the Heat went on to win in overtime. LeBron James scored a game-high 32 points, 10 rebounds, and 11 assists—another triple-double. That loss deflated San Antonio.

"It's by far the best game I've ever been a part of. We saw the championship board already out there, the yellow tape. And you know, that's why you play the game to the final buzzer," James said. "And that's what we did tonight. We gave it everything that we had and more."

LeBron saved his best game of the series for last. No team had won a Game 7 on the road since the 1978 Washington Bullets. The odds were on the side of the Heat. By the end of the third, the Heat were only up by a point. LeBron had four points in the first quarter, but he paced the Heat with 10 points in the second, ending the game with 37 points. The Heat ended up winning comfortably at 95–88. King James brought another title to South Beach and won his second consecutive Finals MVP. It was only the twelfth time a team had gone back-to-back, and LeBron became just the third player to win back-to-back MVPs and NBA titles, following Hall of Famers Bill Russell and Michael Jordan.

"I work on my game a lot throughout the offseason," said James. "I put a lot of work into it and to be able to come out here and [have] the results happen out on the floor is the ultimate."

It was a huge win. LeBron James had shot, dunked, and swatted the Heat to another title. Not only had LeBron continued to dominate in every aspect of the game and keep winning MVPs, but he also made good on his promise to bring multiple championships to Miami. The minute the Finals were over, the term "dynasty" was the only thing that anyone could talk about. And the question became: Could the King make magic happen again next season?

★ CHAPTER TWENTY-FOUR ★

2013–2014

Down to Earth

Since *The Decision*, the Big Three had helped the Heat win 74 percent of their regular season games, but Dwyane Wade was becoming more injury prone and Chris Bosh's play was inconsistent. When the three players came to Miami three seasons earlier, they all signed six-year deals with an early termination clause that allowed any of the Big Three to opt out after four years. The 2013–2014 season was the fourth year of their contracts. A shadow of uncertainty would follow the Heat that season as everyone wondered if all three players would honor the full length of their contracts.

LeBron James dealt with a few injuries, and the Heat ended its regular season with 54 wins and 28 losses. They didn't finish with the best record in the league, but they won enough to earn a second seed in the Eastern Conference, behind Indiana.

The Heat swept the seventh seed Charlotte Bobcats before handling the Brooklyn Nets in five games. They then won a rematch against the Indiana Pacers in the Eastern Conference Championship series by 4–2 to set up a Finals rematch against the Spurs.

The last time these two teams had met, the defeat really hurt Tim Duncan and the Spurs, and San Antonio hadn't forgotten. Statistically, this series was a great one for LeBron. He was the leading scorer for all but one game and averaged 28.2 points per game and 7.6 rebounds for the series despite having cramps that knocked him out of Game 1. The Spurs were an all-time 6-of-6 in Game 1s and they beat the Heat 110–95.

"After I came out of the game, they kind of took off," James said. "And it was frustrating sitting out and not be able to help our team."

The Heat beat the Spurs by two points late in Game 2. Game 3 was a tough game for them. It wasn't that they played poorly—LeBron and Wade both put up 22 points and shot relatively well—but San Antonio had five players in double digits and beat the Heat 111–92.

In the next game, LeBron paced the Heat with 28 points and 8 rebounds, but that night D-Wade was just 3-for-13 and Bosh was 5-for-11. Game 5 was more of the same. The Spurs handled the Heat and killed Miami's hopes for a three-peat. LeBron broke down courtside and began to cry. He had left everything on the court and the Spurs were just better. It forced LeBron to take stock of his career, his life, and his legacy.

★ CHAPTER TWENTY-FIVE ★

2014–2015

Home Again

Four years had passed since he decided to relocate to Miami, and LeBron still thought of Cleveland as home. He wanted his children to think of Cleveland as home, too. He was expecting his third child, a girl, in the fall. Maybe he wanted his baby girl to be born in Ohio like his boys had been. He had always dreamed of bringing a title to Cleveland and breaking the Cleveland Curse. The championships were great, of course, but *The Decision* still haunted him. One of his goals was to win his hometown an NBA title and break the 50-year championship drought that cast a shadow over the city. James had a lot of thinking to do that offseason.

On June 11, 2014, LeBron announced his decision to return to Cleveland in a written statement posted on *Sports Illustrated*'s website—a far cry from the hype of *The Decision*. In his statement, LeBron said it wasn't that he was leaving Miami, but that after four years, it was time to go home.

The Cavaliers had fallen into disarray after LeBron signed with the Heat four years earlier. The team won only 19 games the first year without LeBron. The Cavs did not make the playoffs in any of the seasons without LeBron, but in the 2011 draft, Cleveland selected Duke point guard Kyrie Irving and Texas power forward Tristan Thompson with the first and fourth picks. These two players would end up being vital to the Cavs and begin the rebuilding.

Cleveland's new general manager, David Griffin, had been busy trying to be reload his squad. He had found a new coach in David Blatt (who had coached a number of very high profile teams abroad) and traded future Rookie of the Year Andrew Wiggins to the Minnesota Timberwolves in exchange for All-Star Kevin Love. The trade brought some much-needed firepower to a Cavs team that only returned with Kyrie Irving, Matthew Dellavedova, Tristan Thompson, Anderson Varejão, and Dion Waiters from the 2013–14 season.

The season got off to a great start for LeBron personally, as he and his wife, Savannah, welcomed their third child, daughter Zhuri, days before the first game. And while things got off to a rockier start on the court, by the quarter mark of the season the Cavs were 13–7 and had just won 8 straight games.

After the 8-game win streak, Cleveland lost 13 of the next 19 games, in part because they lost center Anderson

Varejão to injury for the season and LeBron was out, injured. That left the Cavs without their best player and starting center. Their record crumbled from 13–7 to 19–20 in those few weeks. It looked like the Cavs were going to fall apart—until they made some trades. The Cavs brought J. R. Smith and Iman Shumpert to Cleveland. Two weeks later, Cleveland traded two draft picks to the Denver Nuggets for Timofey Mozgov, a Russian center who had played for Coach Blatt with the Russian national team. The stronger roster would also allow LeBron and the other members of his new Big Three—Kyrie Irving and Kevin Love—to focus more at their positions.

LeBron's return and the fresh blood sparked a season-saving 12-game winning streak. A member of Cleveland's Big Three was the game's leading scorer in each game. LeBron averaged over 25.6 points per game during that run.

The Cavs only lost nine more games the rest of the season and went into the playoffs as the second seed in the Eastern Conference. The Celtics were no match for the Cavs in round one of the playoffs and everyone knew it. Unfortunately, during Game 4, some cheap play would change the course of the Cavs' entire postseason. In the first quarter Kevin Love chased for a rebound. To keep Love from getting to the ball, center Kelly Olynyk clamped down on his right arm, pulled down and back. *Pop!* Kevin immediately ran off the floor holding his shoulder with a handful of trainers running after him. He did not return. Shortly after the game, the Cavs' doctors ruled Love out for the rest of the season.

J. R. Smith was later ejected from the game for swinging his elbow, so the team was down two of their key players. LeBron dropped 27 points that game and showed once again that he could handle physical play. The Cavs swept the series in four games.

Kevin Love was back on the bench with his arm in a sling and supporting his teammates by Game 2 of the next series against the Bulls. Down 2–1 after losing Game 3, the Cavs were tied with the Bulls in Game 4 with 1.5 seconds left. LeBron took two steps behind the arc, turned, squared up, and hit a fadeaway three just as time expired. He iced the game! That shot would carry the Cavaliers through the series as Cleveland won the rest of the games to take the series 4–2.

Even the strong Atlanta Hawks were no match for the Cavaliers that year. Cleveland swept the Hawks, and LeBron dominated the series. He was each game's leading scorer and had a game high number of assists in all four games.

While LeBron was resurrecting the Cleveland Cavaliers and leading them to the NBA Finals, another team was developing into an unlikely powerhouse. The Golden State Warriors were led by that season's MVP point guard Stephen Curry and shooting guard Klay

Thompson—the Splash Brothers. Along with Draymond Green, Andrew Bogut, and Andre Iguodala, the Splash Brothers had set records all season. The Warriors started the season with a 24–0 run—better than any team in professional sports history and that included an NBA record 14–0 road start. That season Steph set a record with 286 three-pointers in a season. The Warriors' coach, Steve Kerr, was named Coach of the Year.

The Cavaliers had seen LeBron James usher in a new era for Cleveland, a 20-win turnaround, and LeBron's fifth NBA Finals in a row. But would they be strong enough to defeat Golden State?

In Game 1, Steph put on a show. He would dribble the ball from hand to hand, fall over and throw the ball up mid-fall, and it would still swish. Even the Cavs were wide-eyed with shock. But while Steph and company were playing team ball, LeBron was playing a lot of isolation ball: backing guys down into the paint, posting up, or draining fadeaways. At the end of regulation time, the game was all tied up.

During overtime, the Warriors began making every shot while the Cavs started missing. Kyrie tried to make something happen to help the Cavs out. He drove hard at Klay Thompson and tried to change speed when his leg gave out. Kyrie smacked onto the floor, and he hobbled off the court noticeably limping and clearly angry that his body had given out on a night when he scored

23 points. With Kyrie off the floor, the Warriors could focus on LeBron alone, and Golden State took the first game by 108–100.

Before Game 2, the bad news came in: Kyrie had fractured his kneecap. Anderson Varejão, Kevin Love, and now Kyrie Irving—three starters and two All-Stars—were all out for the season.

The Big Three was now down to just one, LeBron, so he broke out all his tricks. He drove the lane and got smacked in the face by Draymond Green for his efforts. He dunked, shot fades, posted up, and hit skyhooks. It took another overtime period to decide the game, and LeBron dragged the Cavs to victory to tie the series at 1–1.

"I tried to give it all to my teammates. And they do a great job of giving it back to me. Total team effort," said James. "To be back in the same position we were in three days ago and to come back and even the series is big time."

It was back to Cleveland for the third game. LeBron continued to impress. He simply ran by defenders and jammed the ball home. There was no spot on the floor that LeBron couldn't hit from that night, and he helped build a 20-point lead. By the two-minute mark, though, the Warriors had trimmed the lead to one point. But the Cavs bounced back, and moments later, LeBron hit a deep three to put the Cavs up by eight before point guard Matthew Dellavedova threw himself to the floor to gather a loose ball and secure the victory. LeBron had 40 points, 12 rebounds, and 8 assists over 46 minutes of play. He set a record for most points scored in the first three games of the finals with a total 123 points.

Up 2–1, the Cavs were feeling confident, but all the injuries had forced reserve players to start and play more minutes than expected. The Cavs did not have the luxury of a rotation. The Warriors did, however, and their bench was as deep as any NBA team. That depth proved to be too much for Cleveland. The Cavs lost big in each of the next three games. They had left too much on the court and didn't have enough to close out the series. Game 4 was a blowout. Games 5 and 6 were closer, but not by much.

Losing the championship crushed Cleveland. Of course, the fans had fallen back in love with LeBron and understood the reasons for the loss, but they were still heartbroken. They had been so close. LeBron had come home, he had promised redemption, and he led the Cavaliers to within a few games of the title. Yet the team couldn't deliver. In the end, the injuries had been too much to overcome. It was LeBron's fifth straight Finals appearance, but he had only won two. It was time to go back to the drawing board.

★ CHAPTER TWENTY-SIX ★

2015–2016

"Cleveland, This Is For You!"

The team was playing great through the first half of the 2015–2016 season, but there were rumors that LeBron was actively trying to get one of the assistant coaches, Tyronn Lue, named as head coach. The rift between LeBron and Coach Blatt that had started in the playoffs the previous year had only gotten worse. The idea of firing a coach while having the best record in the conference and on pace for a 9-game improvement over the previous season was unheard of in modern sports, but on January 22, 2016, just days before the midpoint of the season, Cleveland fired David Blatt.

General Manager Griffin said that "a lack of fit with our personnel and our vision" was the reason for the firing, but then Griffin announced Lue as the head coach. It looked like LeBron had pushed Coach Blatt out.

After Coach Lue was hired, the team went 27–13 through the rest of the season. By the time they entered the playoffs as the number one team in the Eastern

Conference, the Cavs were playing some of their best ball that season. The Cavs swept the Detroit Pistons in the first round before sweeping the Atlanta Hawks for a second offseason in a row and handling the Raptors in the Conference Finals to set up a rematch with the Golden State Warriors.

These were not the same Warriors from a year ago—they were better. This team had won 73 games that season, breaking the record set by the legendary Michael Jordan–led Chicago Bulls during the 1995–96 season. For many, that made them the best team to ever play together, but the Warriors needed to win the title to complete their amazing season.

In Game 1, the Splash Brothers had an off night, each missing shot after shot, so Draymond Green and the Warriors bench stepped up to help win the game. LeBron and Kyrie were filling stat sheets every game they played, but to win a title, Cleveland would need more than 10 points off the bench (especially considering the Warriors bench scored 45 points).

"When you get outscored 45–10 on the bench and give up 25 points off 17 turnovers, no matter what someone does or doesn't do, it's going to be hard to win, especially on the road," James said.

If Cleveland fans were worried about playing a Warriors team that had shattered records before Game 1, they were panicked now. Losing Game 1 by a score of 104–89 had many fans conceding the series before Game 2 even started. After the second game in Oakland, it seemed hopeless. Golden State stomped the Cavs by 30 points. The Warriors looked unstoppable. It seemed like a foregone conclusion that the Warriors were going to repeat as champs.

Game 3 was back in Ohio, where the Cavs had played wonderfully that season. The Cavs defense was tougher and tighter at home during Game 3. They pushed the ball up the court quicker in transition. Kyrie was hitting from deep, LeBron broke out his skyhook, and the Cavs were up by 8 points at the half. The Cavs had 21 points off turnovers in the first half, despite the Warriors slicing and dicing with great ball movement. J. R. Smith began hitting more threes, which gave LeBron those few inches of space to operate. That was all he needed to make the Warriors pay. LeBron and Kyrie were the two best players on the floor that night, putting up 32 and 30 points respectively. The Cavs ran the Warriors out of the building to the tune of 120–90. Cleveland was absolutely buzzing. Maybe they could beat the Warriors!

Just when the Cavs fans started to allow themselves to hope again, Steph Curry had a monster game. During Game 4, Steph found his range again and went off for 38 points. LeBron had 7 turnovers. In the end, Cleveland didn't have enough to even the series and lost 108–97. One game was all the Warriors had left to win to clinch the title. The Cavaliers had to win three straight games—and no team in NBA history had ever come back from a 3–1 deficit in the Finals. There was zero room for mistakes.

Back in California for Game 5, the series shifted when the Warriors' defensive force in the paint, Draymond Green, was suspended by the league for the accumulation of flagrant fouls. Neither team could build a lead in the game. Back and forth, back and forth the lead went. Also during the game, Warriors center Andrew Bogut went down with a serious knee injury. It was another blow for Golden State.

LeBron and Kyrie each scored 41 points, contributing 82 of the Cavs' 112 points that game. That's 73 percent of the team's total points! James added 16 rebounds and 7 assists to avoid the team being eliminated in a 112–97 road win.

Game 6 was at home in Cleveland. The Cavs lead by as many as 24 points and never trailed in a lopsided affair. LeBron tallied 41 points for a second night and improbably forced a Game 7 after being down 3–1.

LeBron and the rest of the team all packed their bags one last time and boarded the team plane. No matter what happened, this would be their last trip of the season.

The starters played the majority of Game 7 for the

Cavs. They were down by 1 point at the start of the fourth quarter when LeBron changed the game with one play. Steph caught the ball and ran to the top of the paint with J. R. Smith as the only Cavalier back on defense. Steph passed the ball to Iguodala, who tried a layup when LeBron swooped in from out of nowhere to swat the ball. There is no way he should have been able to catch Iguodala and stop that shot, but LeBron James was just that good. The moment became an instant all-time highlight.

With under a minute left, Kyrie sunk a dagger three that capped the game. LeBron hit one of his two free throws to keep his team ahead with a 93–89 lead that would end up being the final score. LeBron had another triple-double with 27 points, 11 rebounds, and 11 assists. He gave his all in those seven games for a fantastic over-all performance that earned him the NBA Final MVP.

And that was it. Cleveland finally had an NBA Championship title. The city's favorite son had come home and redeemed himself and his hometown with the first ever title for the Cleveland Cavaliers. The curse was broken after 52 years! The feeling was incredible. LeBron was so happy that he fell to the floor and sobbed.

LeBron cried out, "Cleveland, this is for you!"

It was the most important championship LeBron had ever won. This one was for his kids, his family, and his friends and neighbors. This was for the community that watched him grow into a pro and then watched him leave for Miami. This was for all those he had hurt with *The Decision*, for all those he let down, for the fans who burned his jersey, and for the kids who cried when he left. This was for his home, where his heart has always been. This was for Cleveland.

"I'm coming home with what I said I was going to do," he said after the game. "I can't wait to get off that plane, hold that trophy up, and see all our fans at the terminal."

LeBron has won every award there is to win. He has three rings, multiple MVPs, and has been an All-Star all but one year of his career. He has been the most dominant player of his generation. One question will always come up: Is he the greatest of all time? To be the greatest of all time, you have to do something no one has ever done before. LeBron brought his team back from the dead to give Cleveland an NBA championship, their first title and the city's first championship in 52 years, despite being down 3–1. No one has ever done that before.

So is he the greatest of all time? He has years of basketball left, but he is without a doubt a part of the conversation. LeBron James is an amazing player, and we are lucky to get to watch him play for the rest of his career.

Look out! LeBron James had a 52-point game during the Prime Time Shootout on February 8, 2003. The Fighting Irish beat Westchester 78–52.

St. Vincent-St. Mary's retired LeBron's high school jersey, #23, on February 24, 2003.

LeBron is poetry in motion as he defies gravity during a layup on February 12, 2004.

LeBron powers up and over the Pistons' mighty defense in the second round of playoffs on May 19, 2006. Detroit won, 84–82.

With the NBA Championship Trophy on the left and the Most Valuable Player trophy on the right, LeBron James wins his first championship with the Miami Heat against the Oklahoma City Thunder on June 22, 2012. Proving that *The Decision* paid off!

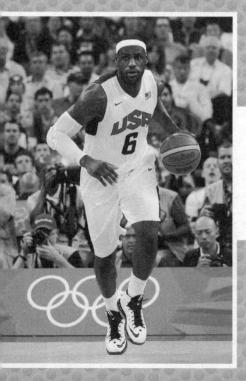

LeBron handles the ball during the 2012 Olympic Men's Basketball gold-medal game against Spain on August 12, 2012, in London, England.

Giving back and helping those in need has always been a top priority for LeBron, whose LeBron James Family Foundation is dedicated to positively affecting the lives of children and young adults through educational initiatives. Here he unveils a legacy project at the Boys & Girls Club in Gretna, Louisiana, on February 15, 2014.

MVP and champion! LeBron (with his children LeBron Jr., Zhuri, and Bryce) during a press conference after winning the NBA Finals against the Golden State Warriors on June 19, 2016.

LeBron James's NBA Statistics

Yr	TM	G	GS	MIN	FG	FG%	3P	3P%	FT	FT%	STL	BLK	TO	PF	OFF	DEF	REB	AST	PTS
03-04	Cle	79	79	39.5	7.9-18.9	.417	0.8-2.7	.290	4.4-5.8	.754	1.6	0.7	3.5	1.9	1.3	4.2	5.5	5.9	20.9
04-05	Cle	80	80	42.4	9.9-21.1	.472	1.4-3.9	.351	6.0-8.0	.750	2.2	0.7	3.3	1.8	1.4	6.0	7.4	7.2	27.2
05-06	Cle	79	79	42.5	11.1-23.1	.480	1.6-4.8	.335	7.6-10.3	.738	1.6	0.8	3.3	2.3	1.0	6.1	7.0	6.6	31.4
06-07	Cle	78	78	41.0	9.9-20.8	.476	1.3-4.0	.319	6.3-9.0	.698	1.6	0.7	3.2	2.2	1.1	5.7	6.8	6.0	27.3
07-08	Cle	75	74	40.4	10.6-21.9	.484	1.5-4.8	.315	7.3-10.3	.712	1.8	1.1	3.4	2.2	1.8	6.1	7.9	7.2	30.0
08-09	Cle	81	81	37.7	9.7-19.9	.489	1.6-4.7	.344	7.3-9.4	.780	1.7	1.1	3.0	1.7	1.3	6.3	7.6	7.2	28.4
09-10	Cle	76	76	39.0	10.1-20.1	.503	1.7-5.1	.333	7.8-10.2	.767	1.6	1.0	3.4	1.6	.9	6.4	7.3	8.6	29.7
10-11	Mia	79	79	38.8	9.6-18.8	.510	1.2-3.5	.330	6.4-8.4	.759	1.6	.6	3.6	2.1	1.0	6.5	7.5	7.0	26.7
11-12	Mia	62	62	37.5	10.0-18.9	.531	.9-2.4	.362	6.2-8.1	.771	1.9	.8	3.4	1.5	1.5	6.4	7.9	6.2	27.1
12-13	Mia	76	76	37.9	10.1-17.8	.565	1.4-3.3	.406	5.3-7.0	.753	1.7	0.9	3.0	1.4	1.3	6.8	8.0	7.3	26.8
13-14	Mia	77	77	37.7	10.0-17.6	.567	1.5-4.0	.379	5.7-7.6	.750	1.6	0.3	3.5	1.6	1.1	5.9	6.9	6.4	27.1
14-15	Cle	69	69	36.1	9.0-18.5	.488	1.7-4.9	.354	5.4-7.7	.710	1.6	0.7	3.9	2.0	0.7	5.3	6.0	7.4	25.3
15-16	Cle	76	76	35.6	9.7-18.6	.520	1.1-3.7	.309	4.7-6.5	.731	1.4	0.6	3.3	1.9	1.5	6.0	7.4	6.8	25.3
		G	GS	MIN	FG	FG%	3P	3P%	FT	FT%	STL	BLK	TO	PF	OFF	DEF	REB	AST	PTS
Totals		987	986	39	9.8-19.7	.498	1.4-4.0	.340	6.2-8.3	.744	1.7	.8	3.4	1.9	1.2	6.0	7.2	6.9	27.2

LeBron James's Year-to-Year Highlights:

2000:
- Ohio State Champions

2001:
- *USA Today* All-USA First Team (first sophomore ever)
- Ohio State Champions
- Ohio Mr. Basketball (first sophomore ever)

2002:
- *USA Today* High School Player of the Year
- Gatorade Circle of Champions National Player of the Year
- *USA Today* All-USA First Team
- Ohio Mr. Basketball

2003:
- *USA Today* High School Player of the Year
- Gatorade Circle of Champions National Player of the Year
- *USA Today* All-USA First Team
- Ohio Mr. Basketball
- Ohio Division II Player of the Year
- Ohio State Champions
- National Champions
- McDonald's High School All-American Game MVP
- Jordan Capital Classic MVP
- EA Sports Roundball Classic MVP
- First Round NBA Draft Pick

2004:
- Bronze Medal, Olympics
- NBA All-Rookie First Team
- NBA Rookie of the Year

2005:
- Led NBA in field goals made (795)
- Led NBA in minutes played (3,388)
- All-NBA Second Team
- Member of the All-Star Team

2006:
- Member of the All-Star Team
- NBA All-Star Game MVP

2007:
- Member of the All-Star Team
- Member of Eastern Conference Championship Team

2008:
- Led NBA in average points scored per game (30.0)
- Member of the All-Star Team
- Member of Eastern Conference Championship Team
- Gold Medal, Olympics

2009:
- NBA Most Valuable Player
- Member of NBA All-Star Team
- Member of the All-NBA First Team
- Member of the NBA All-Defensive First Team
- Named NBA Player of the Month four times

2010:
- NBA Most Valuable Player
- Member of NBA All-Star Team
- Member of the All-NBA First Team
- Member of the NBA All-Defensive First Team

2011:
- Member of NBA All-Star Team
- Reached 500th career block

2012:
- NBA Most Valuable Player
- Member of NBA All-Star Team
- Member of the All-NBA First Team
- Member of the NBA All-Defensive First Team
- The youngest player to reach 19,000 career points
- Gold Medal, Olympics

2013:

- NBA Champion
- NBA Most Valuable Player
- NBA Finals MVP
- Member of NBA All-Star Team
- Member of the All-NBA First Team
- Member of the NBA All-Defensive First Team

2014:

- Member of NBA All-Star Team
- Member of the All-NBA First Team
- Member of the NBA All-Defensive Second Team
- Cavaliers All-Time Assist Leader
- 61-Point Game vs. Charlotte Bobcats–March 3, 2014

2015:

- Member of NBA All-Star Team
- Member of the All-NBA First Team
- Cavaliers All-Time Assist Leader

2016:

- NBA Champion
- NBA Finals MVP
- Member of NBA All-Star Team
- Member of the All-NBA First Team
- Sixth Consecutive NBA Finals Appearance

GET ON THE FIELD, UNDER THE NET, AND BEHIND THE PLATE WITH YOUR FAVORITE ALL-STARS!

Read the entire Great Americans in Sports series by
MATT CHRISTOPHER

LB-KIDS.COM

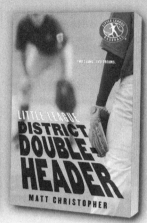

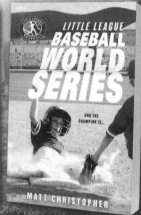